Items should be returned on or before the last date shown below. Items not already requested by other borrowers may be renewed in person, in writing or by telephone. To renew, please quote the number on the barcode label. To renew online a PIN is required. This can be requested at your local library.
Renew online @ **www.dublincitypubliclibraries.ie**
Fines charged for overdue items will include postage incurred in recovery. Damage to or loss of items will be charged to the borrower.

**Leabharlanna Poiblí Chathair Bhaile Átha Cliath
Dublin City Public Libraries**

Baile Átha Cliath
Dublin City

Brainse Fhionnglaise   Finglas Lib
T: (01) 834 4906 E: finglaslibrary@dub...

Date Due	Date Due	
	3 JAN 2(	

D1313359

Published 2016 by
Veritas Publications
7-8 Lower Abbey Street
Dublin 1, Ireland
publications@veritas.ie
www.veritas.ie

ISBN 978 1 84730 651 7

10 9 8 7 6 5 4 3 2 1

Designed by Lir Mac Cárthaigh, Veritas
Printed in Ireland by SPRINT-print Ltd, Dublin

Veritas books are printed on paper made from the wood pulp of managed forests. For every tree felled, at least one tree is planted, thereby renewing natural resources.

For Ann Osborne (1935–2008)
Mother Church, Mother Ireland, Mother

FASTING AND FEASTING

Radio Reflections on Christmas and Easter

Aidan Mathews

VERITAS

Contents

Foreword

E ven in a culture that has become predominantly post-religious, Christmas and Easter remain major celebrations. The time of year, of course, has something to do with their strength of survival. Winter would be harder to endure if the solstice festivities were discontinued, and Holy Week in the Northern latitudes reflects the instinctive thanksgiving of our species as the earth takes heart again in the exhilaration of springtime.

But the respective celebrations of the birth and death of Jesus the Jew, in their bittersweet blend of fasting and feasting, perfectly signify our reverence for the beautiful ordeal of the world, with its precarious fertility and its problematic mortality, while those for whom the Resurrection is the life and passion of the Lord from the point of view of God, are both astray in themselves and utterly at home in the same instant for reasons the rationalists can never wholly construe.

Fasting and Feasting comprises a series of short radio scripts, broadcast at various intervals over the last ten years, on the single subject of the holidays/holy days of Christmas and Easter in the Christian calendar. They are my attempt to revisit the strangeness of the supposedly familiar scriptural accounts of the Nativity and the Crucifixion in the canonical Gospels, but without obsessing (a frequent failure of the tradition, both Roman and Reform) on one or the other narrative to the hurtful detriment of the ordinary teaching and reconciling ministry of Jesus of Nazareth. For the Nativity narratives of Luke and Matthew are paschal portents too, just as the Passion narratives are the climax of the Incarnation.

Aidan Mathews
Into Ordinary Time 2016

1.

Stations of the Crib

I have been fascinated by the report of the census of Caesar Augustus in Luke's Gospel since childhood; in part, this is probably due to the glamour of hearing obscure Latin names and places being read aloud at midnight masses in my parish church by a red-haired priest who had buried sixty Allied soldiers in the sand of the beaches at Normandy in the first hours of the D-Day landings twenty years before. Even now, the phrase 'Quirinius was governor of Syria' evokes beloved memories from the 1960s: headscarves; mantillas; chasubles; bulky adults jamming against my school shorts as I kneeled; a lugubrious organ lurching into a major key; the companionable smell – stout, sweat, socks – of the world before en suites; the sight of altar-cloth tucked into a shirt collar as the paten appeared; and my mother wiping the lipstick from her mouth as she walked up to the altar to the admiration of men.

Now the enrolment of Caesar Augustus hasn't always impressed the scholars as much as it does me. Their consensus is that the census is a con. However they tweak the chronology, they can't align the birth of Jesus the Jew with the immense imperial preparation for a global poll-tax, which is, after all, the necessary narrative trigger for the trip to Bethlehem by Mary and Joseph of the house of David. But the evangelist's strategy here isn't one of reportage. He's an artist, not an archivist. What he wants to do, it seems to me, is to compare and contrast two kinds of book, two kinds of peace, and two kinds of world, in order to summon us into the crisis of choice.

Augustus, who has named the month of August after himself, presides in Rome as the first emperor and as high priest, as *pontifex maximus*, a builder of bridges – a title still preserved, incidentally, by the pontiffs of Western Christianity. He is, in fact, the greatest man in the world. He is even more than that. He is a god. A tactful and appreciative senate has declared him to be divine, a god-man; and his deification has been consolidated by an official cult throughout his enormous dominions. Not until Nazi Germany will so much of Europe come under the say-so of one totalitarian power; and not until the glory days of the European Community will there be so much confidence in the creation of a durable and civic super-state. For Augustus has enforced the *Pax Romana*, the Roman peace – safety, security, and free trade – throughout the Mediterranean regions; Virgil himself, the poet laureate, has written a poem for his immortal patron which is as messianic as anything in Isaiah. Little wonder that Augustus, whose every word is law, whose word is indeed the word of a god himself, determines to bring his realm to book. He will name the world like a second Adam; not only name it, but number it as well. He will register reality. He will sort it all out and sum it all up, sensibly, scientifically, quantifiably, in a catalogue of the contents of creation. On the way, he'll make pots of loot. In short, he'll be an Enlightenment photo-fit.

Luke is a gentile and not a Jew, or, in James Joyce's summary of the fuller and fulfilled man, he is a greekjew/jewgreek. He knows the worth of what we call today his Greco-Roman heritage (a strong argument has been made that he had read or seen the *Bacchae* of Euripides), but he knows as well that behind the *Pax Romana* stand the gibbet and the gallows, the tactical violence of the criminal justice system that dispatched Jesus of Nazareth, the voice, par excellence, of non-violence and reconciliation. What Luke offers instead is the central Semitic insight, at work throughout the Hebrew Bible, that God is among the weak and the broken and the bad, that their story is stronger than the silence of state history, and that the tale of an individual family may say more than a statistician's transcripts about the shalom of Emmanuel.

So a girl of twelve or thirteen, a girl of marriageable age, a girl called Maryam, rests against fodder in some makeshift encampment, and flicks the stub of her nipple with her finger till it stiffens. A baby's mouth closes on the brown of her breast.

When my daughter Lucy was little she used to play with the figures in the crib. At the time we had only the basics: Jesus, Mary and Joseph (in that invincible order), plus Isaiah's ox and ass. Over the years we increased the manifest until it looked like Noah's Ark. Shepherds, kings, camels, cocks, hens, angels, mongrels, and, most recently, a pig. All of this was due to Lucy's initiative years before when she climbed up on top of a turf-basket and contributed to the crib a Sylvanian family, several Smurfs, Super Grover from Sesame Street, a metallic koala from a keyring, and two toy German soldiers with flame-throwers. Saint Francis, the installation artist who designed the first crib, would have been quite happy with the theology implied by this bunfight. So, I imagine, would Saint John Paul II, the Bishop of Rome in Lucy's infancy, who, when he gave Holy Communion to Ferdinand and Imelda Marcos in the Philippines, was signalling the Jewish revelation that God's hospitality is limitless, that it reaches beyond Judas at the Last Supper even to you and me in the here and now, and that the baby in the manger, the child in the feeding trough, who displayed such humanity over thirty years, that it strikes us as godly, giving us food – and drink – for thought.

Because we've lost faith in the state of being adult, we tend to idolise childhood, so it's a case of women and children first as the culture's morale capsizes. In John Milton's marvellous 'Hymn on the Morning of Christ's Nativity' the poet pictures the entire pagan pantheon – Baal and Moloch and Osiris – in a retreat or rout as the new Christian order commences. But the mystic John Moriarty (and my daughter Lucy) know the truth of it: we must commune together or consume each other. When the Christian princes of America and Britain talk of pre-emptive strikes and the death penalty, it is time to remember the breaker of bread from the badlands of Galilee.

I'd always assumed that the account in Matthew of the Wise Men – or the Magi, as we know them best – was a theological parable, a midrash, without any historical basis. But my cynicism vanished on reading an account of how, on the death of a Dalai Lama, Tibetan Buddhist monks risk darkness and snowstorms to search for his reincarnate self in some newborn baby or infant and, finding such, bring him back with them to the monastery. At about the same time, I discovered that two of the most important theologians in the Catholic Christian tradition are, well, Kaspar and Balthasar.

Older by far than the feast of Christmas at the winter solstice, the Epiphany has been treated sumptuously by generations of artists, and I love especially the works in which worldly patrons have insinuated their own fleshy likenesses into the features of the three kings. By contrast, the face of the child Jesus is often wizened, almost geriatric, weighed down on Day One by his destined part as the second mask of the Blessed Trinity. Even the little Christ in my family crib forty years ago was a plump twenty pounder, at least three months old, watched over by a Scandinavian Madonna who looked very like the blonde singer in Abba. But I happened upon my favourite representation of the birth at Bethlehem some years ago in Paris. The young girl lies stretched out on the ground, her head on her wrist, her lips puffy and gashed, watching in a tired and tender way the skinned seal pup in the lee of her lap. It is for this that the Wise Men from the east, in an early Easter reconnaissance, have followed 'nonsense' in place of sound navigation, a new star instead of a fixed one. It is to this they bow down: to the simple ensemble – at once historic and prehistoric – of the human family.

Could it be that a later Christian legend-upon-legend has long imagined the Magi as a trio because of the three women in the Gospel of Mark who carry funerary spices and embalming fluids to the tomb in which the body of Jesus has been hidden? The Wise Men too bear gifts: gold for a king, frankincense for a priest, myrrh for a petrified corpse. So the symmetries of folklore would insist that the wood of the crib and the wood of the cross are carved from the same renewable sources of human pain.

Then let the star these watchmen follow be a yellow star, the star of David, star of the scapegoat, the star that the Bishops of Rome forced their Jews to wear at all times as a mark of marginality, and which the Third Reich revived across Christendom when the Beatles were babies.

I always had a soft spot for Joseph, the father of Jesus. Perhaps this is because I spent a large part of my childhood in the company of older persons whose small-talk was wise and often mischievous and whose smells were already ancestral. We walked together at the same intended pace in Donnybrook and Wicklow, discussing the War of Independence and the Civil War and the war to end all wars. When these personages were no longer spoken of in dispatches, I presumed they were dead, just as the Gospel citations of Joseph end in the death-certificate of total silence. Stained glass windows in odd churches around the country do depict him sinking wistfully in quite modern beds with sheets, blankets and bolster, while an androgynous Jesus looks on respectfully; but this is wishful thinking. We know next to nothing about him.

There's the tradition, of course, that he was a widower, providing Mary's child with the stepbrothers and sisters who are called the siblings of Jesus in the scriptures; the tradition too that he was a carpenter – a belief that mutates magnificently in Martin Scorsese's film *The Last Temptation of Christ* into a shot of the young saviour fashioning commissioned crosses for Roman crucifixions. A revisionist alternative sees Joseph as a luckless cuckold, pictured in many Renaissance paintings sitting cross-legged, vexed and perplexed, outside the barn where his bride has just given birth. But he is not alone. A Catalan crèche in Barcelona, for example, will always feature a fellow squatting to defecate in a corner of the crib as a symbol of the quotidian human mess that the Incarnation embraces. Although Christians – and Muslims everywhere – revere the virgin birth, Joseph's perplexity mimics the slow, stalled manner in which we actually encounter mystery.

Why then would a man of such mettle as the theologian Karl Barth salute Joseph? It is surely because of the saint's discernment, the way he works through perturbation towards clarity. In Matthew's Gospel, those periodic dreams that direct him – first to fidelity, then to a fugitive life, and, finally, in the fullness of time, to a return to his origins – enhance his status by associating him with precedents in the Hebrew Bible, but Joseph's real grandeur springs from his actual abandonment of self. The word that comes to mind, travestied as it has been in the Western press this past while, would be the one which signifies submission, openness, complete receptivity to the will of God. In short, the word 'Islam'.

My first child was born in a snowstorm on the winter solstice. Soft wet petals fattened against the window of the men's room in the maternity hospital like the slick flakes of cherry blossom in the month when she had been conceived. Japan had come to the Coombe to remind me that light is the order of the day.

'Whenever I have a child, I get sympathetic haemorrhoids from pushing,' said the man beside me.

It was a long labour, eighteen hours in all. My wife inhaled the gas with the gusto of a cocaine addict. Snow fell like confetti at the glass. I walked downstairs through the Christmas decorations to smoke on the steps outside. Where was the Latin-American novel I had brought with me?

Once, years before, I had passed a woman in labour. Her lips were bleeding. 'Jesus, Mary and Joseph, I'm dying,' she cried; but she was bringing life into the world. And I had heard of a woman in a cottage hospital who had cried out in the direction of the night-light as she died, 'Jesus, my waters are breaking.' But she was dying. Our lethal birthings; our vital deaths. Truly we are stranger than our own gods.

In the hospital chapel new mothers were nursing beside the crib. We sneer at churching nowadays, but the primal rite – to be found in the Book of Common Prayer – is heartfelt thanksgiving that a woman and child have survived the horrors of labour. No wonder that, in Second Isaiah, the prophet envisions the Creator in the pain of process when he has the Lord exclaim: 'I will cry out like a woman giving birth.'

The head appears. My wife rests. The head rests. Now she is my Queen of Diamonds, two-headed, doubled, different, dear. A form flows out of her. It is my daughter, thirty today and a woman who is going out clubbing as I speak this sentence. I hold her as the snowstorm whines. She is my branch. She is my root. She is very scrunched.

Our car has been vandalised. Two portholes have been smashed in the windscreen. The two front seats are as white as vestments. The shaver I used to shave my wife's legs only a week ago has been stolen. But the radio works. It plays Harry Belafonte. He sings to the snow and the snow flocks to hear him.

There was a Christmas morning years ago when I crept home in the small hours, stepping on grass and not on gravel for fear of waking my father, tiptoeing close to the side of the staircase nearest the wall lest the wood of the banister wheeze. The tree in the living room had filled the house with the odour of forest. My brother's light was still on. I went in to him.

'Happy Christmas,' I said.

He had been dying for many months. The tumour in his brain had grown again; slowly, subtly, incessantly. I suppose it was the size of a boiled egg or a Brussels sprout, just as it had been before. He could no longer stand or speak properly. His eye was rigid and unblinking, set in a bloated, balding head. He had been helped downstairs the day before to see the lights on the tree, the dachshunds at his slippers.

'You too,' he said.

I sat down in the sick bed-smell of his room. I had been with my girlfriend, and her scent was all over me: my hands, my face, my hair.

'I like to meet her,' he said. 'I look forward.'

What I wanted more than anything was to lie down beside him, and hold him, and tell him he was dying, because nobody had. But all I did was to walk the nails of the fingers of one hand very shyly across the white underside of his wrist where the sleeve of his pyjama had been pulled up. His body was warm from the blankets; mine was frozen from the bike. We had never been so close. We had never been so distant.

'Shell me about her,' he said.

The whole host of heaven lit up the sky outside. It was only the light from dead stars. Another, later Christmas, my father would be watching them as well when he died, after a late-night television programme on the migration of birds, sitting upright in the same armchair where he had once filled in the census forms of a modern Caesar Augustus; and, in due course, I would watch them too from the bullet-proof windows of the closed ward in a psychiatric hospital, where I had been for so long I had forgotten what clothes I came in.

'Shall I leave the light on?' I said to him, as I got up to go.

'Leave ith on,' he said, and waved to me. 'Leave ith on for the time being.'

Our Lady – sometimes invoked with scandalous indecorum as the BVM, as if she were a computer or a car – remains in my life as an icon, in the more modest sense in which that term is used by the Eastern Orthodox tradition; but she entered it as an idol. Her cult influenced my whole life when I was small, and I am ashamed now to admit that I always found it both beautiful and benign.

It was dismantled in less than ten years by the nomenclatura of the day, and the model they have put in its place – of a dogged and indomitable readiness to receive God's word and God's will – is all agape and no eros. When I make a May altar for the table in our hall, my children are touched by me and not by it, for I am seen to be ethnic to the point of being exotic. Yet I remember when a courtly and chivalric feeling for Our Lady was as natural and as national as rabbit ears for a television set; and, in the moonlit nights of my adolescence, I would always remove my miraculous medal, rusted from years of baths and showers, and hang it on the bedstead before I settled myself, arms crossed on my chest like the effigy of a stone crusader on a medieval catafalque.

Christmas is Calvary for an awful lot of people. But that isn't a paradox. It is a direct parallel. In English, after all, bedlam is a short form of the word Bethlehem, while the trial and the dying of Jesus spell out in forensic detail what it is that Law and Order does on a daily basis, here and everywhere else, to protect the peace, for the short form of Jerusalem is traditionally Salem. So the cross shows us the double-cross of culture.

The shepherds who visit Mary in the stable are not stand-ins for King David, the prototype of the pastor. In Luke's time, they were seen instead as desperadoes from a sordid underworld, vile criminalised individuals. So the stable is an unstable venue, reversing our priorities. The whole of Western philosophy begins with the self; but the stable knows that it starts with the Other. We all talk about bringing Christ into the world; but the stable knows how this is done: in darkness, in displacement, in the mess and mucus of jeopardy. Her afterbirth steams in the dirty straw. The incense of the breath of livestock fumigates her. She bites through her own cord in the manner of mammals everywhere. The bandaged infants pulls at her.

2.

Waking a Jew

Palm Sunday

Holy Week in the Christian calendars (for there are more of them than ours alone) gets off to a very strange, even a very false, start by proclaiming one or another of the Gospel accounts of Jesus' entry into Jerusalem. In each version the itinerant teacher from the hillbilly badlands of Galilee rides on a donkey into the holy city to the almost idolatrous acclamation of his faction. They carpet the route with their own clothing. They shout out the same slogans of devotion that had rung in the ears of Alexander the Great when that very different demigod thundered through the same gate three hundred years earlier. They behave, in general, with the same violent enthusiasm that can characterise spellbound groupies at stadium rock concerts; for fascination of that order is, after all, the etymological origin of the word Fascism itself.

In short, this is a triumphal march, a royal procession, and was understood as such by General Allenby who, when he approached Jerusalem by the same route during the Great War, dismounted his horse and proceeded on shank's mare

23

to his next war conference, as an act of pious deference to his Supreme Commander. I know this only because I was in love with Lawrence of Arabia when I was a little boy – short-sighted and without spectacles – squinting at the blurred figure of Peter O'Toole through the tiny perforations in two Marietta biscuits.

Yet if the evangelists' depiction – rapture, unanimity, branches of olive and palm – were true, it would be the grand finale of a fable, and not the bare, bleak beginning, of our reportage. For the Passion narratives are tragic prose before they are redemptive poetry. In fact, the word tragedy itself, as the great anthropologist and theologian René Girard used to remind his students, comes from the Greek *tragodos*, the road of the sacrificial goat; but though the sound of the term is Hellenic, its stench is the same as that of the scapegoat in the Book of Leviticus. Indeed, it's the culture of Jerusalem and not the city-state of Athens that enables us to talk about such things in the first place, because it's the Hebrew Bible and not the Greek classics that really understand the dialectic of violence, victims, and keeping the peace.

So the crowd – in Latin the *turba* (Girard again), from which the words 'disturb' and 'perturb' are derived – is both an honour-guard and a jeering gauntlet. It is, genetically, a mob; from *mobile*, meaning changeable, volatile, a coinage of the poet Ovid, the master of metamorphosis. It is certainly the same crowd that will instantly reject its matinée idol in the plaza before Pilate's official residence, for it is human nature, be it Jewish or Irish, that a crowd swerves between love and loathing, between desire and resentment, until the white-haired boy becomes a bogeyman, the lamb of God a black sheep, the halo a noose, the platform a scaffold, and Palm Sunday turns into Passion Sunday.

The steep, hero-to-zero demise of today's celebrities has a clear trajectory: first we divinise them; then we demonise them. First we turn them into Gods; then we kill them for being all too human.

The pantomime of the donkey-ride darkens into parody when the Roman militia ridicule Jesus by dressing him in the same imperial purple of our priests' vestments during Lent. It may be argued that the churches continue the soldiers' prank by foisting anachronistic forms of kingship on a figure better understood in less archaic images. Admittedly, the democratic process doesn't favour the Lord, either. It is Barabbas – called Jesus Barabbas, Jesus the Son of the Father, in ancient editions of Matthew's Gospel – who upstages his non-violent namesake as the people's choice. When it comes to granting clemency, a terrorist-turned-politician is a much safer bet than a queer, counter-intuitive, skid-row sort.

The Last Supper
The Last Supper is often spoken of as the first mass, though the mass – and any service of Eucharist in the Christian traditions – is more than the mere re-enactment of a meal shared by a scared coterie in a rented room in Jerusalem during Passover. It narrates instead a panoply of events and beliefs which move from the victimised to the vindicated Jesus in a classic Judaic defence of the wronged innocent, a habit of advocacy which began, centuries before, in the first book of Moses with the brothers Cain and Abel.

25

The Eucharist is a mystery, but it is not magic. Christianity, like Judaism, deplores the paranormal and its grotesque voodoo, preferring by far the down-to-earth supernatural, which is to say: the presence of God in the ordinary universe. This was not always clear to me. When I was small, my mother and I would queue for Holy Communion in the stuffy aisles of our parish church and we would wait to kneel at the marble altar rails that divided the chancel from the nave, the sacred from the mundane, the priest from the people, as decisively as the Berlin Wall bisected the communist East from the consumer-driven West. My mother would wipe the lipstick from her mouth, out of respect for the Man Above, and I would tuck the starched altar-cloth into my shirt collar out of reverence, lest any subatomic particle of the blessed bread miss my tongue when the priest with Parkinson's disease picked a quivering wafer and aimed it at me.

If only my chivalric, Iberian sense of the body of Christ in the unleavened button of bread had been matched by an equal awareness of the body of Christ in the dying celebrant who gave it to me, in the wall-fallen congregation on the creaking kneelers behind us, and in the newspaper sellers in the street, covering the accusatory trash of the tabloids with cellophane when it lashed outside. It would never have occurred to my scrupulous mother, peace be upon her, that she and her children too were part of the flesh and blood of Jesus in the world, and that whether the second person of the Blessed Trinity has one nature or two is a less pressing affair than our attempts, by giving and forgiving, to imitate Jesus of Nazareth, and so accomplish some small part of the will of God, which is the law of love and not the love of law.

The ordinariness of Eucharist goes even deeper, as only ordinariness can. It is rooted in two primal and prehistoric actions: the telling of stories and the sharing of food. Just as the sharing of food transforms an act of survival into the mealtime of community, so the telling of stories transforms our solitariness into social identity. When Jews celebrate the Passover, just as Jesus the Jew did throughout his short life, the house liturgy of the Seder isn't simply an affectionate reminiscence of the time when the Lord delivered the House of Jacob from the land of Egypt. It is a deep communion with the timeless and eternal foundation of their faith as a chosen and covenanted people. It is more even than a participation; it is a partaking. Likewise the Lord's Supper, with its Aramaic imperatives – This my flesh, this my blood – when Jesus offers himself as a model not of reprisal or retaliatory violence for his own murder but as an experiment in reconciliation that excludes nobody, his own betrayer included.

The Criminal Justice System
The commencement of the legal year in this country is marked by a mass which members of the judiciary and the Law Library traditionally attend, the Catholic and apostolic judges – one imagines – in search of wisdom, the Catholic and apostolic barristers in search of wit. I had a great uncle who was both a piously Irish parish priest and a British military chaplain at the battle of the Somme, dodging shrapnel in his officer's uniform as dying

teenagers from a dozen different countries screamed for their mother, their *mutig*, their *madre*, their *mere*, their mams, mums, and mamas; so I have a robust sense of irony. But there is something breathtaking in the sight of those who groom and safeguard the justice system, the privileged civil service of revenge and retribution, doing homage at the cult of a condemned criminal; a working class redneck with an accent so rough the onlookers thought he was calling on Elijah, the prophet, when he was calling on Eloi, his God.

Robert Brasillach, a forgotten Vichy minister who was hanged by De Gaulle after the liberation of France, had a somewhat similar sense of irony on death-row in the hours before he was executed in the presence of a priest. His poem '*Le jugement des juges*' [The Judgement of the Judges], inverts the typical courtroom dynamic, crowding the dock with the portly and comfortable worthies who routinely condemn the accused and endowing the bench with the dingy underclass Jesus liked to drink with.

Of course, Brasillach's insight is only half-true. He remembers, as René Girard would often remind students in his seminars, that the Greek word *Paraclete* in the Gospel of John, signifies a legal defender, someone who springs to our assistance at all times, but he forgets that the word Satan, from the Syriac *Satanas*, means a prosecuting counsel, a persecutor. He forgets, in other words, that the bi-polar world of blind justice is grounded in the same system that slaughtered Jesus, in the same complicit understanding among all the authorities of Church and state, that a little regulated violence is better than the possibility of unchecked mayhem. So prisoners sit in the stench of their own faeces in barred cells, remand inmates hang themselves with dreary regularity, and any custodial term, whether its duration be a year, a month, or just a week, becomes a life-sentence in a culture of stone and of stoning, where the tabloids sell in their thousands outside places of Christian worship on the Lord's day.

Judaism magnificently compressed its whole ethics into love of God and love of neighbour. Radical Judaism, or Christianity as it came to be known in the backstreets of Antioch, set a head-spinning standard when it called for love of enemy as the only way out of our doomed, retaliatory civilisation. As an old Yiddish couplet has it, 'When chimneysweep and baker fight, baker turns black and sweep turns white'; thus the course and consequence of conflict cancel all our differences at the very moment when we think we have nothing in common, and the hectic increments of obsessional hostility pile up to the point where the death of our adversary, or his disappearance, visits us more like a bereavement than an orgasm.

Two thousand years ago a Jewish holy man, whose love of Torah made him exceed it, spoke of forgiveness, spoke of non-violence; and the community he founded has been busily rationalising and reducing both ideas for about the same length of time. Forgiveness has become so intellectual that Pope John Paul II could pardon his would-be assassin from the heart, but Mehmet Ali Agca stayed shut in a jail called Queen of Heaven, for deliverance to the captives is now a metaphor and not a mandate. Non-violence too was known to be nonsense centuries before the Christian extermination of the Jews of Europe showed us how, if the television cameras are not present, the passivity of the victim only inflames the blood-lust of the executioner. Yet we remain convinced that the two acts, forgiveness and non-violence, are the true divine presence in our DNA, the stardust in our calcified bone marrow.

Jerome, translating the Jewish and Christian scriptures into vernacular Latin for his great Vulgate Bible, was dismayed by John's account of the woman taken in adultery. Surely its mercy was beyond the beyond. The text, which is pure and cleansing, must be imperfect or corrupt. Palestine in the first century of the Common Era would have been like New England under the Puritans, or Ireland, North and South, in the 1950s: Taliban territory. So Jerome included the story as a footnote only. Something in all of us prefers the statutes of the Law to the literature of freedom that the Gospels inaugurate. But if the anecdote of the failed stoning is indeed a footnote, it is small-print that repays close reading.

The Crucifixion

Mel Gibson's 2004 movie *The Passion of the Christ,* which was torture for many audiences, provoked so much small talk and big talk that I can't resist offering my denarius' worth. It seems to me that much human evil – atrocity, pogroms, the black mass of ceremonious capital punishment – is often lacklustre stuff, a routine, administrative, sterile, scheduled turnover. I imagine that the crucifixion of Jesus of Nazareth was altogether more tedious and less theatrical than Gibson supposes. What does make it different, however, from any preceding brutality, is that it has been reported entirely from the point of view of the victim and not of the victimiser. Every moment in the process of persecution and punishment has been magnified by a theological loyalty to the innocent casualty as a new category in human thinking. The violated, vulnerable Other has come into plainspoken sight from its dogged roots in the Hebrew Bible.

Luke, my favourite evangelist, has no interest whatsoever in the idea of atonement, and, as an ordinary Christian, neither do I. Instead, the Passion narratives always and everywhere affirm that God is a saviour, with less operatically gorgeous *grand guignol* than the motion picture moguls attest; they announce that God proclaims an inexhaustible outreach to the lost and unlamented of human history, the detritus in the pit, by refusing to relinquish a single life to the domain of death and obliteration and cultural taboo; they assert that God's hospitality places Jesus, as the embodiment of his ethical Word to us all, at the very heart of heart-broken divinity, thereby merging the physical and the metaphysical, the sacred and the profane, in a vital unity newly understood; which is why, I take it, the Temple veil is symbolically torn apart at the moment Jesus dies.

When I visited Mount Athos for Holy Week a quarter of a century ago, I was struck for the first time by the imperial character of the portraiture of Christ in the Orthodox tradition, in the stern, smoke-blackened icons of the Byzantine Godman. I missed immediately the human, the humanised, the humanistic images of Jesus which are the amino acids of the Western enlightenment, and which capture – and liberate – across the centuries the wounded

31

form, the misunderstood face, the excluded figure, of all those folk who haunt the shadow-lands of society. In a text beloved of René Girard, Jesus asks the demoniac in the cemetery what his name is, and the poor possessed individual tells him: 'My name is Legion, for we are many.' This stumbling shambles is indeed plural: he is the Jew, the dyke, the kike, the kook, the wop, the wog, the knacker, the homo, the abortionist, the arms manufacturer, the Israeli, the Arab, the paedophile, the priest. He is whomsoever we scapegoat in order to safeguard ourselves. Yet we must beware: as the legend of Veronica's veil reminds us, the face of our ironic God will inevitably be the image of the human person we have most despised.

Perhaps that's why the Passion narratives may be said to have fomented the form of the novel itself, and why the emergence of that literary genre in the vernacular languages of Europe chimed with the translation of the Hebrew Bible and the Christian New Testament in the Reformation period. For the characteristic hero of the novel is the misunderstood individual whose travel is also travail, who begins in the asymmetry of abandonment and exclusion, and who journeys from vilification to vindication, through the solitary stations of his destiny toward a shining renewal of community at the close. So the literature of the early modern period is not the opponent of *lectio divina*, of strenuous sacred reading, any more than the university is the opponent of the monastery, but is instead its close and cherished offspring.

The Resurrection

When John Paul II visited Ireland in 1979, it was a little like Palm Sunday all over again. To be sure, the pope arrived as a *deus ex machina*, a god in a helicopter, and not as a side-saddle bohemian; but the results were largely the same. Just as the Jesus movement went to ground during the quick crackdown following the Passion in the mid-first century, so the institutional Christian churches in Ireland, especially my own tradition, blanched at the millennium following the news of abuse scandals, as mentors were revealed as tormentors, and our pieties and practices dwindled into Pavlovian tics. Perhaps this is how your typical East German apparatchiks felt in the early 1990s as they grieved in the aftermath of the sudden disintegration of Communist structures and symbols they had supposed were everlasting. Many Catholic Christians throughout this country find themselves now between dying and rising, in the Holy Saturday space of a claustrophobic decomposition. If the Resurrection of Jesus is the body of Christ that we call the church, then 'risenness' is a much more intermittent matter than we had imagined.

As it happens, belief in resurrection or, more precisely, a personal afterlife, forms no doctrinal part of the Hebrew Bible itself, neither the Law nor the prophets nor the writings. It occurs for the first time in the Maccabean chronicles, within one hundred and fifty years of the life of Jesus and his great rabbinic contemporaries, and it will be a further thousand years before Moses Maimonides lists the conviction in his summary of essential Jewish beliefs. Additionally, Christians assume a rather Gentile understanding of the notion of the hereafter. They assume that eternal life, which is a strictly Semitic concept, is the same as immortal life, which is a Greek notion. But the encounter of the self and the Other can only occur after the annihilation of the ego.

We do not desire resurrection for ourselves. We desire it for those whom we love. We stand into a wardrobe to inhale the scent of a dead spouse from a shirt he wore and didn't wash; we spend Christmas in a Muslim country to avoid the memory of a daughter who died when our hands smelled of resin from a shedding tree in a car-boot; we kiss our blinking parents on the forehead, just above their oxygen masks. But death and rebirth aren't only Omega moments. Our children die as babies and return as toddlers; die as toddlers and come back as Junior Infants; sink and strengthen, subside and soar again, bud and bleed, with their grandmother's smile and their great grandchildren's hair. A separated woman finds happiness after years of marital horror: that is resurrection. A son speaks to his father after forty years: that is resurrection. I myself am a dead man come to life, with a tag on my wrist from the labour ward and a tag on my toe from the mortuary. I have seen so many persons rise from the tomb that it beggars all the sane and silly *son et lumiere* of Saint Matthew's imaginings at the close of his Gospel.

I think often of a disturbed old woman in a psychiatric hospital who wrote in her own faeces on the wall of her room the words: *God is Love.* She too was one of the women who brought the news of the empty tomb, the Easter opening. For the story of the Resurrection is, quite literally, an old wives' tale, God's gossip, brought by those who had come up from Galilee with Jesus and had spent their whole time looking after him. In the oldest of the Gospels, which is Mark's, we meet these disciples, Mary Magdalene, Mary the mother of James, and Salome, at the original ending of the text, at chapter 16, verse 8, long before a bogus supplementary section had been added on in a different style by a different hand to finesse the conclusion theologically. I like it because the Greek version embodies such hard, heartfelt things: trauma, incredulity, hope. 'And they went out and fled from the tomb, for trembling and astonishment had come upon them; and they said nothing to anybody, for they were afraid.'

We too should be scared out of our wits by what we are remembering during these days.

3.
Facing East

I'm just old enough to remember the phrase 'perfidious Jews' in the Good Friday liturgy of long ago or, more precisely, to remember my father's dislike of the expression, which was removed, along with the more vengeful psalms in the priests' office, around the time I walked to the altar as a first holy communicant, closing my eyes and sticking out my tongue at the scintillating pellet. That was the time of the Cuban missile crisis. Now, in a new century, I'm still young enough or youthful enough to learn that the dreadful polemic against the Pharisees in particular, and the Jews in general, which we encounter everywhere in the Gospels, reveals less about the dialogue between Christ and the radical intelligentsia of his age than it does about the bitter struggle between Jewish Christians and rabbinic Jews for control of the synagogues in the decades after the death of Jesus.

This is not a cavil, let alone a censure. Whenever the Church challenges violence, its own or that of others, it is proclaiming the core value of its founder and his own Judaic faith: outreach to the shunned and the scapegoated; the rehabilitation of those who have been despised, defeated and deleted from the community. When we meet at mass to tell stories and to share food, we know that the Eucharist is itself a sanctification of the victim in his suit of spittle and saliva, of one who has been caricatured by public opinion, the law courts, the Church authorities, and the demonic tabloids of the Law. We know as well that everyone in the congregation is more mongrel than thoroughbred, both victimised and victimiser; that we are whole enough in our senses to see that we are fractured in our being; and that attendance at a communion service ought to be a form of social disgrace because it manifests our complete dependence on others and on Otherness in a culture that craves autonomy with attitude.

This is not religiosity. Religiosity is when I spent Holy Week in a monastery on Mount Athos thirty years ago, swooning at the dark didgeridoo sounds of Orthodox chant, when I ought to have been home in Ireland, cleaning either end of a brother who took a thousand days to die of a brain tumour. Religion, on the other hand, is when the six o'clock service turns, through the gift of our own stress and distress, into a Last Supper, when the man presiding over the bread and wine in the closed ward of the psychiatric hospital is himself in pyjamas, and when our inseparable brethren at an AA meeting drink from the chalice as they sip their teacups.

For we too, the perfidious ones, are the Resurrection of the Lord.

There's a moment in Luke's Passion narrative when the Lord has been chiding and/or counselling the women in Jerusalem who are breaking Jewish law by bewailing a condemned man, and the gentle, gentile evangelist brings forward the two thieves whom Augustine famously transmogrified into a cautionary double-act with his 'Do not presume: one of the thieves was damned; do not despair: one of the thieves was saved'. But it's not the elegance of an ancient admonition that interests me now, though it did once. Instead, it's the Greek verb Luke uses to describe the fate of these two convicts that I find fascinating: '*anairethenai*' means to 'be done away with, to be finished off, to be annulled'. The term is redolent of the bad breath and disinfectant of bureaucratic slaughter, and its casual, clockwork brutality perfectly epitomises the blood and barbed wire of the twentieth century, the midpoint of which bloodbath was my birthplace.

The starting pistol of the hundred years' homicide which became a genocide was probably the revolver shot at Sarajevo that signalled the start of the Great War in the year of my father's arrival in the world; and when he eventually left, eighty-three years later, Sarajevo was still on the front pages. In between, I had shouted courtesies at my deaf grand-uncle, a boyish padre at the Somme when half a million lads became cadavers in one day; I had trotted contentedly in the slipstream of sun-tanned ex-servicemen whose erotic prestige derived from the teenage Japanese and Germans they had machine-gunned overseas; I had inspected camp tattoos under cufflinks and costume jewellery; and I had added up, on a cut-price pocket calculator, the piled millions of men and women whose skeletons proliferated like root-work in the soil of Mother Russia. No wonder Marc Chagall's melancholic painting of *The White Christ* re-doubles our dismay, for the crucified Jesus in the midst of the massacre of Jews is both an image of the suffering servant of Israel and, at the same time, the implacable emblem of hard-hearted, historic Christendom doing away with, finishing off, annulling.

One painting is not, of course, the whole picture. Insofar as we can recoil from violence, we have copied the reflex from the example of the Hebrew Bible and the Christian New Testament. The original audience for the Iliad was enthralled by killing, just as the modern multiplex viewers of *Die Hard* are both aroused and appeased by retribution. If we can transmute that gusto into disgust, we have made a start. But our venal civilian lives are a battlefield too, and even our virtues can defile us. Out of the blinding savannah we stepped one hundred thousand years ago, astray in our own strangeness, with our opposable thumb, our perfect teeth, our skull-shattering tomahawks; and a hundred thousand years later, only our teeth have had to be replaced.

One of the most striking features of the post-Resurrection narratives in the four canonical Gospels is that there's no talk of retaliation. Fear, yes; perplexity, misgiving, joy and ecstasy, yes; but no mention of revenge or vendetta. In most mythology, and much literature, this is precisely the point in the plot at which a Galilean underground cell should rise up against its murderous enemies – Pilate, the High Priest, and their parties – and avenge their crucified leader, or, in modern terminology, seek justice, a Latin word for getting even through the liturgies of public vengeance in the law courts.

Jesus and his followers bypass all of this. They have entered a green venue, a new place. They are not united 'against', as most of us are. They are simply united. They are at one. But we do not have to wait for the Resurrection to be sure of it. The Passion story itself is a Resurrection account, because, being told from an Easter perspective, it completely vindicates the scapegoat at its centre, and demonstrates a saving God who sees persons on the periphery of the human order as constituting the centre of the divine one. So the Greek verb for being 'raised up' refers both to the cross of execution and to exaltation in heaven.

In the Gospel beloved of the Orthodox churches, the Gospel of John, the divine Jesus presides over his butchery like a priest presiding over the mass. But in the synoptic Gospels, especially in Matthew's, which the Latin Church has cherished, Jesus is a casualty and not a choreographer. He is the miscarried human Messiah. He is the Son of God, but this is an honorific title and not a theological definition. He embodies the Word of God, but he is not the incarnate Logos. Such talk belongs to the next three centuries, and would make no sense to him. At this moment, he has no adjectives. He is completely alone. None of the evangelists will say that he has died. It is too painful. Instead, they speak of a last breath, a stale final exhalation.

It will become the wind of Pentecost.

※

Saint John's account of the raising of Lazarus intrigued me when I was small, partly because I'd seen pictures of the event in a few of my godfather's art books and had also watched it occur for real in a black and white Bible movie in our own living room. For a decomposing Egyptian mummy to have staggered out of a sandstone tomb at the say-so of the Lord seemed to me to be a prestigious feat and I couldn't imagine why the other three evangelists had omitted to mention it. I now appreciate, of course, that the story of Lazarus dovetails reportage and parable in a typically Johannine manner. Its truthfulness is more than tabloid headlines. In addition, what had always appeared to be a prelude to the Passion, a warm-up act, so to speak, is the very reverse. The story of Lazarus shows us, with Semitic strictness, what the Resurrection is not about. It is not about a cadaver on walkabout. It is not about the Night of the Living Dead. It is about the God of the living who has set his heart on us and will have us for himself.

Oddly enough, the Resurrection wasn't a problem, intellectually or emotionally, in the past. Aquinas thought our dogs would be with us in heaven, and nobody laughed at the time. The crucifixion was the stumbling block. Early images of Christ on the cross obscure it behind the majesty of his pose. Jesuits instructed the Japanese in the teachings of Christianity without dragging Calvary into their classes, because Orientals found such details revolting. Today, the reverse applies. The Good Friday ceremonies at Easter are sometimes better attended than the vigil mass on Holy

Saturday, and this is because ordinary Christians and post-Christians can identify more easily with horror than with happiness, with desolation than with deliverance. Resurrection means nothing to many of us.

The Jews of Jesus' time were no different. Over the previous two hundred years, belief in a personal afterlife had taken root for the first time in a people already profoundly religious for centuries; but many still demurred. There was much discussion and debate. Presumably the parents of the future Messiah shared the hope of heaven and handed it on to their child. As it happens, all of the Pharisees strongly supported resurrection from the dead, though the Sadducees mocked the notion as infantilising nonsense. It is in this argumentative context that John's tale of the tomb might caution us. God is not a cosmetic mortician who resuscitates stiffs. Resurrection is deeper work than that.

There's no account of the Resurrection in the four Gospels. It's an event that lies beyond the modest dimensions of time and space, beyond the mortal calendar of our world, in the deep prerogative of God. What the evangelists offer us instead, in the multiple levels and layers of their sedimentary meditations on the meaning of Jesus and the traditions about him, is an extraordinary sense of the aftermath, of Easter exhilaration, of the literal enthusiasm – a Greek term meaning 'the god in us' – that seized his friends and strengthened swiftly into a Semitic sense of 'God with us', of Emmanuel.

Women are the first terrified witnesses. Women fashion the human future out of their flesh and blood in the Eucharistic mystery of their bodies and, as such, they are more hospitable to the strangeness of being and becoming than those who reason and rationalise. But the men do follow, and the great Gospel texts that attempt to represent their blurred vision, their burning hearts, their blundering minds, recognise too that language cannot manage such complexity. So the stumbling, fumbling, vulnerable contradictions in the four Gospels perfectly reproduce every individual Christian's struggle to understand that the crucified Jesus is the risen Christ.

Perhaps that's why I'm so fond of the story of the two men walking to Emmaus in Luke's Gospel, their footloose, footsore journey that's also listed pithily in an addition to Mark. The narrative is a guide through grief, after long reflection, into an enriched sense of possibility. But I love as well the warm plurality of the Gospels, the four and not one, their diverse and alternative conversations. Some of us are sustained by Mark, some of us by John. Just as the different Christian traditions vary in their charisms – the Methodist from the Roman Catholic, the Presbyterian from the Baptist – so the four versions of the Gospel message offer us four individual pilgrim paths to a place where the Lord is risen and the tomb is empty now because we are the body of Christ.

In 1942, around the time my parents were on honeymoon in a hotel in Kerry that was full of vacationing priests, a Nazi mobile extermination squad entered a small village in the Ukraine and machine-gunned its Jews against the whitewashed wall of a latrine. One of them, however, a cantor in the synagogue, asked permission to pray before he was murdered, and he sang the Shema, the morning and evening creed of Judaism. The Germans liked his strong tenor voice so much that they brought him along with them when they left. In the evenings, when their gun-barrels were cooling, they would lie in the grass and listen to him intoning portions of the synagogue service or crooning Yiddish love songs. Sometimes they'd find a raft or a rowboat and push him out into the middle of a lake so that his voice would travel clearly across the glittering acoustic of water. Jesus the Jew did the same thing in Galilee to make sure he'd be heard by the crowd on the shoreline.

I'm not a combat veteran, of course, but at times I feel like those soldiers of the Reich: corrupt, contaminated, yet nostalgic for the priestly tone, the paternal timbre of a secure religious childhood that's ages removed from the secular resentments of middle life and the competitive cruelties of peacetime. My generation is hitting sixty now. We've lived in the city and the suburbs and we know that the world of the water-sprinkler and of Neighbourhood Watch is every bit as brutal as a battlefield. Desire and resentment, random and routine, radiate everywhere. When we recognise how compromised we've become, we blame it on the children. If we'd had no family, we could afford to be generous.

And yet; and yet. For the answer doesn't lie in the Santa spirituality of our childhood, in the cardboard Christ of our kindergartens. Infancy can be infantile, and often is. Childhood can be childish. What I would wish for myself and my generation this Easter is not renewed belief but the final, lethal unbelief in the God who never grew beyond six or seven in our lives. What we need is a God who is adequate to our appointments and our disappointments too. What we need is an inner Easter, a personal death and resurrection.

Bertolt Brecht famously advised us to forget about the bad old days and get on with the bad new ones. But I'm old enough to have survived two models of Church – the council of Trent and the second Vatican council – and to have witnessed in the transition from one to the other the complete dismantlement of a fifteen hundred year-old cult of Our Lady in less than a decade. I'm not going to compare the world of the parish sub-deacon with the world of the parish subcommittee except to say that human nature doesn't change. We will always prefer power to authority. Perhaps that's why none of my friends has a Bible on his bookshelves though they're all seekers after truth. It's never because they think the doctrine of the Trinity is Pythagorean claptrap; it's usually because they were hurt or humiliated by a professional Christian when they were little.

I love my faith more than my nationality, but I'm not blinded. The string quartets are moving into the sanctuaries now in the service of the lesser god of culture. The feet are washed but the bread is not broken. Only our parents are immortal anymore. Institutional Christianity is dying in Europe, a continent that, in spite of smartness and social gaiety, has stopped reproducing itself out of a deep misgiving about the future or, in Biblical terms, out of a lack of Resurrection faith. The God of America is not the God of Exodus or Easter but the Supreme Being of an eighteenth century caricature. So the torch is passing to Africa and to Asia: not only, as they say, to a Christian Africa or to a Christian Asia but also to an African Christ and to an Asian Christ, where the dialectic of Peter and Paul, of tradition and daring, can dizzy us again.

We may think, in other words, that we are performing the paschal mystery of passion, death and Resurrection; but it is the paschal mystery that is transforming us.

4.

Grace at the Solstice

Christmas can be Calvary. In the first Station of the Cross, Jesus is condemned to death. In the first station of the crib, Mary discovers that she is pregnant.

Herself only a child, she is immediately condemned at one and the same instant to the tiny lethal life imprisoned within her and to a capital charge of immorality under the ancient decency laws of the state. In the Taliban badlands of a pre-modern culture, obsessed with purity and pollution, she is surely the most vulnerable human person on the terrible, retaliatory horizon: an unmarried mother, a fallen woman, an abominable, liable thing. She can be buried up to her uterus in the ground and pulverised with stones the size of tumours until she looks like afterbirth.

In the second Station of the Cross, Jesus is given his cross-beam to carry to a garbage-dump where he will asphyxiate gradually in the long labour of his dying. In the second station of the crib, Mary accepts her predicament.

Affliction becomes a difficult gift in the trusting presentation of the past to the future as the utter initiative of a saving God, for midwinter's deepest secret is the solstice, and this is Mary's darkest day. From the moment her period has stopped, possible bloodshed by brutalised policemen or by indignant vigilantes begins. But the oddball deity of her people is partial to those in dire difficulty. She has listened long enough to the scripture readings in her Galilean synagogue to have learned that, in amongst the cultic abracadabra of the Temple traditions, there is another voice, the mysterious, migrating whisper of a Lord who is both older and younger than the many other man-made gods of the Bible.

When, in the book of Genesis, these criminal divinities, these 'Elohim' as the Hebrew calls them in a plural noun, cry out atrociously for the blood of the boy Isaac, it is this queer, non-violent interloper called Yahweh who will stand with Abraham and with his descendents against all human sacrifice, and take the side of victims in a world of victimisers.

In the third Station of the Cross, Jesus falls for the first time. In the third station of the crib, Mary carries Christ for a first full trimester.

This is the earliest age and stage of her vigil, an Advent not as spotlight or as searchlight but as silence and as secrecy and as sedimentation; Advent as a fast and not a feast. The thought of the gravity of the Law may still terrify her in the small hours, but the law of an even greater gravity embeds her in the grind of time, an anticlockwise grounding in minutes and hours and infinitesimal nights, duration as endurance.

In the fourth Station of the Cross, Jesus meets his mother. In the fourth station of the crib, Mary meets the supportive totality of the nurturing culture that has fathered and mothered her.

Just as she will wrap her baby in the swaddling clothes of the legendary stable, so too she has been dressed and decked out since her naked birth in the rich familial fabric of her Jewishness, layer upon layer of its wholeness and holiness, in what the scholars speak of nowadays as the 'social imaginary'. Christians think of John the Baptist as the biblical intermediary between the two religions, but it is Mary for me who embodies the plenitude of patient Judaism. Thus, in the very Gospel that is often accused of anti-Semitism, which is the book of the apostle John, the dying Jesus commends parent to child and child to parent – 'Woman, behold your son. Son, behold your mother' – in a bond of reciprocal love.

In the fifth Station of the Cross, Simon of Cyrene helps Jesus to carry his load. In the fifth station of the crib, Joseph helps Mary to bear her burden.

We know as little of the one marginal figure as of the other. The stories we call scripture illuminate their hands and not their faces, leaving obscure the small historical services of passers-by who did not pass by, of bystanders who stood their ground. Indeed, in the canonical accounts of Saint Mark and Saint John, a deep indifference obliterates the figure of Joseph almost altogether, just as neither evangelist signals the remotest interest in the fabulous oral traditions of the birth of Christ in a hovel in Bethlehem.

We must look to Matthew's mythical description of the origins of Jesus of Nazareth as a sort of Moses Mark Two to discover, amongst all his creative accounting, a preoccupation with preoccupation itself. Just as later Renaissance frescoes will always picture Joseph at a moody distance from the mother and child in the bedlam of Bethlehem, he is already far away in his fragmentary imaginings. He is lost in his thoughts. He is in another world, and it is the real one, the one that ages us, the one in which we finally assume flesh, the world of risk and responsibility.

What will he do? What is his response to Mary's Magnificat, which is also her minority? The complexity of choice and the anguish of indecision are marvellously represented in the nightmare dreams of her sweetheart as he tosses and turns in bachelor horror. What now? What next? What then? What if? This tumultuous interior to-do, this turmoil of desire and aversion, is everybody's crisis when mercy and morality collide.

If Matthew's fables sketch the silhouette of a step-father, it is Luke who has modelled the Madonna. In the sixth station of the cross, the legendary Veronica wipes the forehead of Jesus, and the smeared likeness of an ordinary human face replaces the blank sheet of the Temple veil torn in two. But the actual Luke, this extraordinary artist of the compassion narrative that is the life and death of Jesus, has fashioned two of the three most genetic images in the wistful Western world; for, after the sign of the crucifixion itself, nothing is more powerful – because more powerless – than the motifs of the Annunciation and the Nativity; and they are masterpieces beyond Michelangelo himself, the narrative miracles of the only Greek evangelist, a man whose Mediterranean civilisation stressed a kind of trinity too in the simultaneity of the good, the true, and the beautiful.

Now in the seventh and in the ninth Station of the Cross, Jesus falls a second and a third time; but 'Don't stop, Daddy. We seen that page!' my three year-old daughter told me on her first Good Friday outing in our parish church two decades ago; so I shall pass from the seventh and the ninth station of the crib, which are the second and the third trimester of a pregnancy in all its painstaking and its patience, in all its mortal precariousness, to the tenth milestone of cross and crib in which Jesus is stripped of his clothing on Calvary hill and Mary is made utterly vulnerable as her waters burst and her contractions deepen in a galvanised outhouse.

This is childbirth in the hostile, inhospitable world before obstetrical sterility and safe anaesthesia. It is therefore death-defying; it is often death-defeated. Small wonder that Medea, the mother who murders her offspring in a drama by Euripides (a playwright whom, incidentally, Luke will quote in the Acts of the Apostles), should tell her Athenian audience five centuries before Christ, that she would rather face carnage on the battle-field than the cruelty of child-bed, because the solitariness of birthing is worse than any trench warfare.

The eleventh station, so, is the fullness of time. Jesus is nailed to the cross; Mary labours alone among the companionate animals at the radical source of the whole story. After all is said and done, it is down to her, the crux of matter itself, the rainbow curve of the female pelvis, entrance as Exodus, the arc of our species stretching from its humble hominid beginnings in the family of mammals to its present preternatural status as the most unearthly earthlings of all, the stars of Planet Blue.

Jesus dies with a large and inarticulate cry from the wooden cross. Jesus is born with a little, inarticulate wail in the wooden stall.

It is the close and the start of the heart's concerto in the exhilarating torment of a universe we must undertake and undergo without ever fully understanding. It is the twelfth station. It is you and me, here and now, now and again, a speaker listening to a listener speaking, our differences so similar that we are intimate aliens and alien intimates, the living image of each other's strangeness, two incomparable copycats in the mystery of encounter, finite and indefinable.

But who in the thirteenth Station of the Cross takes Jesus down from the ghastly masthead?

The same persons who put him there in the first place, I suppose, will later depose him: which is to say, it will be the likes of ourselves, the scum of the earth, the ring around the bath, swineherds and shepherds, casualties who forget in our innocence that we are culprits too, culprits who forget in our guiltiness that we are casualties as well; in short, the loveable ramshackle lot of us, not forgetting the potentates, the wise men, the magi, the grim intelligentsia with their academic credentials who bring their gold and frankincense to the great ideas, to the abstract nouns, to the glittering institutions, and who read King Herod's massacre of the infants as a figure of speech and not as a fact of life in a world where the unborn and the newly born have died in their unbearable multitudes.

In the fourteenth Station of the Cross, Jesus is laid in the sandstone tomb. In the fourteenth station of the crib, Jesus is laid in a dispenser bin.

All of this food for thought is holy in its way; some of it may be silent or at any rate speechless, for that is what infant means in Latin; little of it could ever have been calm as the quaint, narcotic carol tells us. The brightness here is midwinter light, a slender silver lining, grace at the solstice.

Blessings on the brat in the barn. He will never feature in the census of Caesar.

Good wishes to you and yours at Christmas.

God's wishes for Christ's mass.

5.

Laments into Dances

Four years ago and for the first time in my life Easter came so early that Good Friday fell on the Feast of the Annunciation, which is the twenty fifth of March. There was nothing that could be done about it. Holy Week is moveable because it derives its dating from a Judaic lunar calendar, but the date of the Annunciation is fixed and it has to be. Once the primitive Christian community decided to mark the birth of Jesus during the pagan festival of the winter solstice in late December, the logic of the literalists determined that Mary's adolescent uterus must have quickened exactly nine months before, around the aptly vernal equinox, when the winter stirs towards birthing.

This co-incidence of the two liturgical dates hadn't happened since the start of the 1930s, and, after its scheduled occurrence in the present year, it won't be witnessed again for well over a century. Now celebrating a feast (the Annunciation) on the very same day that you commemorate a fast (Good Friday) is an odd business, a mix of christening shawl and burial shroud, the more so if the feast marks the legendary beginning of a pregnancy and the fast honours the last, legal stages in the public execution of the same embryo as an adult person. No wonder the plus sign in the window of the do-it-yourself pregnancy kit looks a little like a cross. Perhaps it's a Christian joke. Perhaps it's a Christian judgement that we're a dying breed whose beauty is bound up with our brevity.

To talk in those terms is to enter into the bifocal world of paradox. John Donne, the seventeenth century priest and poet, adored being paradoxical. To be honest, it was his passport into the smart set. So it's not at all surprising that, when the Feast of the Annunciation fell on Good Friday in the year of Our Lord 1608, Donne sat himself down to write an ingenious verse on the subject. The myth of Christmas and the history of the crucifixion cross-pollinate quite prettily in his rhyming couplets. This double day, he tells us, in 'Upon the Annunciation and Passion Falling upon One Day', is

... this doubtful day
Of feast or fast, Christ came, and went away.
This Church, by letting these days join, hath shown
Death and conception in mankind is one.

I can see the Dean of Saint Paul's, as he was at the time, posting manuscript copies to his literary pals. Complex and contradictory thinking thrilled John Donne.

But our own contemporary sense of the usurpation of the facts of Easter by the fantasy of Christmas is altogether more sombre than it seemed to the clever dicks we call the metaphysical poets. If in the fullness of time the Jewish Passover, the sacred meal which was eaten yesterday, mutated into the Mass, the ritual remembrance of the passion and death of Jesus among his scriptural entourage, Easter itself has been 'passed over' in the twenty-first century of the common era in an irony that is probably divine. The same Christian supersessionists who proclaimed the redundancy of Judaism for two thousand years have been superseded in their turn by the rise of a post-religious reality in which the holy days have become holidays and the holidays bank holidays and the bank holidays breakaway weekends.

More poignantly, the historical core of the story of Good Friday has been entirely eclipsed by the truthful fable of the Nativity in the Gospels of Matthew and Luke, such that Christmas, that tantrum of waste and haste with its Coca Cola Santa Claus and its Dickensian bric-a-brac in which we infantilise our lives in order to deflect the darkness of the Northern hemisphere, would strike any visiting Martian as the primary rite of Christianity, although the tale of the birth of Jesus was obviously fashioned as a stations of the crib, an abridged children's version of the terrible Passion narrative. And that description of the death of Jesus in the four canonical accounts, which is always part reportage and part reflection, has been further distorted both by occasional Christians and by philosophical professionals whose post-conciliar Easter emphasis, a travesty of the modish Enlightenment myth of irreversible progress, obscures the centrality of suffering by reducing the dynamic double helix of death and resurrection to a linear transcript of what happened before and what happened after.

But the logo of the Logos is not the empty tomb. It is the paschal debacle. It is the cross. That is to say: Christianity is exhilarating, but it is not hilarious. It is the festival of the misfit and the carnival of the failure. We are optimists, yes, but we are tragic optimists. We are hopeful, but we are not full of hope. Each day we cross our hearts and hope to live. We are called to keep faith with the pain of Creation and the anguish of the Creator in the mysterious birthing of the future. We are delivered into, and not out of, our human nature. We are not required to become partly divine; we are invited to become fully human. We are summoned to this world and not to the next. We are asked to affirm the heroic materiality of things. We are asked to grieve decisively for the liminal and for the eliminated. We are asked to choose eternal and not immortal life, not the spirit's survival in some flickering future state but the complete vindication of the person as the masterpiece of God.

Christianity is not primarily a religion of the Book, as Islam and the evangelical fundamentalists understand it, or even of the Jewish Law in a drastically simplified, post-synagogal précis of the strictures of Torah. Strictly speaking, it isn't a religion at all insofar as it tends to identify all official cult as mere cultural product. In many crucial and excruciating ways, it is an anti-religion, a critique of all the human forms of faith from a prophetic perspective which recognises that religions generally decay into religiosity, that icons deteriorate into idols, and that aesthetic ritual degenerates into ritual anaesthesia. It urges agile vigilance against all human gods, especially the gods of reputation and status. The tribe into which I was born worshipped a monstrous two-headed god called Law and Medicine, but the pantheon of phantasmal deities is legion.

That is why the early Christians were accused of being atheists. They understood that the life of Jesus was the death of God as we had imagined him. They understood that the resurrection is the life and death of Jesus from the point of view of God. They saw that we can know nothing at all about this God, but that we can recognise in the ministry and the martyrdom of one controversial Jew something deeply agreeable to the enigma we identify as eternal love. We cannot stare straight into the solar eclipse of that God, but we can glimpse its gist and graciousness in the pinhole of a particular Palestinian life and death. We can even talk about that life and death in the phosphorescence of metaphor. When we do so, we forget entirely that we are talking of mysteries we cannot understand in terms of realities that we can, and that, at least in part, the Lord Jesus sits at the right hand of the Father in our theological imagery because, in the Middle Eastern culture Christ inhabited, the dominant right hand was the social instrument of all hospitality, while people wiped their bottoms with the sinister and stigmatised left.

I have Jewish friends who await impatiently the advent of the Davidic Messiah, the hero, the humanitarian, the historic one. He will rejuvenate the Creation. Everything will be all right suddenly and Semitically.

I have radical friends who await impatiently the advent of a political utopia, of an Ology or an Ism that will galvanise the planet. Everything will be all right and all revolutionary.

I have secular friends who await impatiently the advent of the universal enlightenment, when scientific rationality will finally overwhelm religious superstition, and everything will be all right and all reasonable in horizontal, humanistic light.

We Christians stand instead by the side of a man impaled on a stake in a rubbish dump outside Jerusalem. It is that simple.

I have friends in the arts and in the arts councils who await impatiently the advent of universal literacy and third level education, an era when everybody will have a large paperback library of the best European poetry, be able to play the upright piano at least to Level Eight, and parade in the priestly Tridentine credentials of the creative artist. Everything will be all right and all rewarding.

I have professional friends in hospitals and consulting rooms who await impatiently the advent of the reign of sexual joy as the only antidote to neurotic violence. In this historical climax, everything will be, I suppose, gastronomically orgasmic.

I have friends in the courts who are convinced that if the criminal justice system only victimises victimisers and only violates the violent that there will be peace and plenitude on earth. They forget the deep prudence of all jurisprudence.

We Christians stand instead by the side of a man impaled on a stake in a rubbish dump outside Jerusalem. It is that complicated.

I have friends who are free-marketeers, liberals and libertarians who await impatiently the advent of economic globalisation and the festive obesity of the goods that are gods. Everything will be all right and enriching.

I have militant feminist friends who await impatiently the advent of a social Eden in which the good forces of oestrogen will defeat forever the malign energies of testosterone, and everything will be all right and obstetrically sterile.

I have Roman Catholic friends who await impatiently the triumph of their particular doctrinal tradition, because they confuse Western Latin Christianity with the Kingdom of Heaven. Everything will be all right eschatologically.

I have friends, in other words, who have seen a light in the East, a star shining, an Easter radiance, an earth-shattering cavity in the ground that looks like a stellar impact, the crater of a meteorite.

They want the world to be all Christmas and no Calvary, all Easter day and no catastrophe, all star and no disaster.

They are in thrall, these friends of mine, to one policy, to one programme, to one project. They are enthralled by the one and only answer to absolutely everything. Afterbirth in a barn and a corpse on a cross can mean nothing to them.

We Christians sit in the bodily smell of our churches and we listen Sunday after Sunday to the same enormous, inordinate words from the sanctuary: joy, hope, peace, love, faith. Often we do not feel any of these things. We feel grubby and compromised. Our lives are both scrutinised and obscure, both trivial and afflicted. We live in a world that homilies do not always reveal and liturgies do not always embody. We take our handbags to Holy Communion for fear of pickpockets in the pews. What we experience as hope is very often hypothermia, a consolatory paralysis, the sensation of warmth and well-being that floods the body in the final stages of frigidity.

We forget, God help us, that only the psychopath has peace of mind. We forget that holiness is not happiness, that anxiety and exhaustion and fearfulness are profound spiritual states pervaded by God. Instead we listen to the eirenic sirens of serenity (and sometimes the claptrap of charlatans) who tell us to live in the moment, when we are called as human beings being human to inhabit the crisis of time. For we have not chosen the civil smile of the Buddha but the skeletal grimace on the face of a sanctified criminal.

You who are listening, look up from your hands. If you cannot look up, look around. If you cannot look around, look down at your feet, at those two angular oddities that we wash on Holy Thursday, when the rite divines and discloses within the prosaic solidity of awkward flesh a fragility that is almost thalidomide. Looking down at our feet is an act of depth and detail. They have brought us this far. They were already footsore in the uterus, their soles criss-crossed with isobars. It is true that they deserve better. It is true that they deserve other. But all around us, April is doing what April does best. She is proliferating. Life is fragile because it is fertile. We are fertile because we are not impregnable. We are pregnable because, thank God, we are not pure.

Therefore touch wood. Smooth or splintered, it is the wood of the cross which is the wood of the crib as well. It is the wood of the tree of life and of the good grief of being here. We cannot see the tree for the wood, like the poet Dante at the midpoint of his pilgrimage. But we can hear the birdsong. It is territorial and threatening and very beautiful.

Take a deep breath. Breathe in; breathe out; breathe on. Be barefoot. Stand your ground.

I touch my forehead, the electrified lobes of my brain, where the firestorm starts. I touch the useless nipples of my body that is much more ancient than my human nature. I touch my solar plexus, the sink below my stomach that links me to my mother, she to hers, hers to another, and so on down the long descent of ancestry to the earliest annunciation on the African savannah.

I make the sign of the cross on this Good Friday.

6.

Messenger Boys

When I was a little boy, I slept on the edge of the bed to leave room for my guardian angel.

In the winter months of the world before central heating had been heard of, I sometimes made the supreme sacrifice and pushed the hot-water bottle away from me reluctantly into the middle of the mattress, where the pee of a whole childhood's bed-wetting had produced a stain like a Rorschach map of Ireland without the six contested counties, the same as the weather chart on the new national television station at Montrose. My angel would have folded his wings there like a brace of ironing boards and was celestially comatose, I suppose, with his sleeves crossed on his chest in the shape of a crucifix, the same as my own two goose-pimpled elbows on the cold side of the sheets under the sash window.

I say *he* and *his*, of course, because it never occurred to me that the beautiful hermaphrodite who rested at my right hand during the hours of darkness was fundamentally feminine. Not that he was brutishly masculine, either. He was just generally male, boy-soprano style, with long hair on his head and nowhere else at all, especially in the prohibited zone my mother called the body's Greek and Latin bits. Besides, the Angel Gabriel in the Piero della Francesca print of the Annunciation above my wooden bed-stead, which had come as a gift (gilt-frame and postage extra) with some greeting cards that were painted by foot and mouth instead of by human hand, was much better-looking as a beau than as a belle, whether in 1455 when the artist first imagined him in Arezzo, Italy, or five centuries later in 1965 in Donnybrook, Dublin, when I couldn't imagine anything more real and more radiant than the apricot breath of my sweet, supernatural partner on the other half of the grubby rubber pillow.

For that matter, Piero's imperturbable BVM behind the Roman pillar in the same portrait isn't exactly a pin-up Madonna. She who will be gravid is already grave at the news of it, the debutante is maturing prematurely into a dowager as the first intelligence of her mystical dignity sinks in; and I had to turn away from the cubbyhole in Nazareth to Botticelli's *Birth of Venus* – hanging, as it happened, in reproduction on the far side of the same boy's bedroom beside a bookshelf full of two-and-sixpenny Puffin paperbacks – to see a woman more beautiful even than Sophia Loren or Audrey Hepburn: the Virgin Mary without clothes soaring out of a sea-shell on a strand with all the wistfulness and modesty of a maid, let alone a maiden, still less a sovereign lady in pearls of great price, the Queen of Heaven and Star of the Sea. As the priest who taught me Religious Knowledge would put it in the same late 1960s that the Mass broke suddenly into spoken English, 'We are safe in assuming Our Lady was simply stunning.'

Times change and changes temper us. A happy childhood is a poor preparation for adult life. The body may still be a temple, but it is no longer a church, thank God; and the pure, imperfect relationships that sustain us sacramentally can embody benevolent bed-fellows stranger than any angels. Yet there's no getting away from a wing and a prayer, the wild-goose ghosts who mind us, especially at that eligible season of the solstice in December when more modern messengers – like the angelic *Guardian* newspaper, say – seem insufficient somehow to the depths that surface in our heart of hearts as we inhale the odour of forest in our living-rooms and the scent of straw in the crèche in the hall.

After all, old-fashioned angels are everywhere in the Christmas texts. Their sorties whiten and quieten the whole story, for *listen* is an anagram of *silent*. In Luke's signed version, they buttonhole Zacharias in the Temple, leaving him suitably speechless. Downstream they will croon as one, a barber shop chorus from the blue beyond, to the subhuman shepherds on the commonage where the Christ is born. In the rippling meantime, they pay court with a diplomat's gentility to the Mother of God as she darns a woollen sock with the little walnut mushroom neither of my adult daughters could identify in the toolbox of their frugal forebear, a Fitzgerald from Cobh that was once called Queenstown.

In the case of Mary's sweetheart and suitor, of course, the angels' advent is nearer to a sheer night-terror than to any visionary flashpoint in a festive siesta, for the three obsessional ruminations of Joseph in the Gospel of Matthew – whether to stick with an unmarried mother in the lethal living-space of imperial Palestine, where to hide for the sake of mere survival and when, if ever, to come home again, home again – inscribe all the blind-sided insight and hindsight, the fright and flight and eventual standstill of intricate ethical decision. If we can squint through these magical squadrons to study the mystery of human discernment as it actually unfolds in the solitude of choice, we will find that both evangelists, Matthew the Jew and Luke the Gentile, have fashioned their amazing metaphoric porters (in modern Greek, by the way, 'metaphor' is now the word for luggage-handler) with one point in mind; and that point is almost a nutshell of the New Testament, the very ground-note of the Good News. *Mé phobou. Mé phobéthés.* Do not be afraid.

That is the greeting and the true farewell and the universal password of these extraordinary emissaries. Don't be afraid. Don't be afraid of me. Don't be afraid of God. Don't be afraid of yourself. Don't be afraid of being afraid. That too is all right because trepidation is a spiritual virtue and not just a mood-swing to be medicalised. Or, to use the ancient Attic term for fearfulness, that matches some lost Aramaic original in the oral tradition of such encounters with the eternal, don't be phobic. Don't be phobic like the desolate Virgin Mary in the nineteenth chapter of the honourable Koran who shrieks in the grief of labour, 'I wish that I were dead and my memory blotted out!', or like the hysterical strife of man and wife-to-be in the second century Infancy Gospel of Saint James where, in a gloss that dramatises Matthew 1:19, the carpenter's shame at his ugly engagement to the pregnant singleton erupts in disgust and in misogyny:

'Do you realise how much you have degraded yourself?'
Mary wept bitterly, saying, 'I am pure. I have not slept
with a man.'
Joseph said to her, 'Then where did this creature inside
you come from?'
But she told him, 'I swear by the living God that I do not
know.'

Coming as he did from the metropolitan culture of multiple
gods in the pagan Mediterranean, Saint Luke, who quotes
from Euripides in the Acts of the Apostles, would have
understood the contagion of religious panic. Even the Jews
in their monomania about a singular Lord had only risked
a glance at God's backside on Sinai, from fear of being
vaporised in some thermonuclear meltdown. According to
the classical model, the meeting of mortal and immortal
would always climax catastrophically. Collisions of that kind
were in fact the full-tilt theme of Ovid's *Metamorphoses*, a
work of spectacular overkill and macabre jollity which, by
serendipity, its author dedicated to the emperor Augustus at
around the same time that efficient potentate was planning
the poll-tax and the population-count which brought
stability to the world by doing the very reverse and instead
bringing the world to a stable.

It's even possible that Luke had heard of Ovid's
miscellany. Certainly he knew the legends that were listed
there abundantly. They were, after all, the convertible
currency of a whole civilisation, the household pottery of
the mind's mental furniture in late antiquity. Essentials of
the typical transformation in this homicidal litany include:

boy or girl meets a god, that god rapes and plunders (and impregnates), be it in the alias of a bull or a cob or a cannibal pack of beagles, and this atrocious travesty abolishes the basic humanity of his or her victims, such that they mutate immemorially into animals, vegetables and minerals. They become bears, boulders, stars, store-cattle, rattle-snakes, shrubs, conifers and monoliths, outcrops of mica schist that mimic statuary, carrion-crows, creepy-crawlies, quivering riverside reeds; in short, little, subsisting holocausts that haunt an absolute line of separation between up there and down here, between heaven and earth, between slobber and helium, between divinity and ordinary beings.

However they dwindle or diminish, however the punchline in the poetry distorts their mortal forms with the penalties of presumption, these visited individuals begin as entities and they end as objects. 'The gods are come down to us in the likenesses of men!', cries the crowd in Luke's missionary sequel to his life of Jesus, as they mistake Paul and Barnabas for Zeus and Mercury; but the third evangelist knows that we reciprocate their descent in the likenesses of beasts.

Consider Luke's counter-truth, his Gospel truth, his gentle, Gentile tale of the Annunciation told in the Pygmalion category of fable to an audience that cannot otherwise become a prayerful congregation alert to the utter interiority of the things that matter. Here there is no voracious Jupiter or petulant Apollo to prey upon a target; there is neither seduction nor seizure. In place of the psychotic violence of the pantheon, there is only a transcendent presence so reticent and so respectful of the individual human person in her particular freedom that any overture is almost oriental in the elaborateness of its courtesy and its courtship through the formal tenderness of a trusted intermediary who offers obliquity and not obliteration, the protocols of graciousness.

To be sure, there can be pagan vestiges in the Jewish-Christian perspective. In the parasitic pseudo-scriptures of the second century, a sceptical obstetrician called Salomé inspects the Virgin rather too cheekily on Christmas Eve, and the fingers of this Doubting Thomasina burst into flame – into Greek fire, you might say – to rebuke her flagrancy. But to quit the awful apocryphal writings for the canonical works is to retrieve, again and again, the deep sanity of the emblematic repertoire in the texts we rightly venerate.

Luke the evangelist, Luke the ev-angelos, Luke the good angel, could not have imagined the costly posterity of his courier Gabriel; could not have imagined that the heraldry of his Annunciation would inform the social practice of the Western world and the template of its tact, inspire the cult of courtly love and the savoir faire of sweethearts everywhere; soothe and sedate a fanatical jihadist like St Bernard as he touted total war against the infidel, festoon the churches of Christendom with what must be, after the ubiquity of mother and child, its single most beloved Marian motif, or cause a Christian kid in a dormer room in Dublin during the Kennedy years to move over in the bed and let the light lie down beside him in the darkness.

7.

Criminal Justice

In a childhood that becomes clearer and clearer to me as it drifts into the reminiscent distance, there were always women at the foot of the cross, as all the male evangelists manage to acknowledge; or, at any rate, there were always women at the foot of the stations on Good Friday in the loud emptiness of the parish church in the age before the first public address systems, when the priest had to shout the Good News, sergeant-major-style, so that its gladness seemed grumpy and even grim to the twitching children in the congregation.

Mostly it would be the housekeeper in my boisterous family home, a tireless twenty-something who had joined us as a teenager from a nearby orphanage and remained among us as the ordinary angel of our infancy and adolescence to provide us – and our posterity too – with a model of mother-love, a poignant glimpse of God. But I did the fourteen stations with my taciturn dad as well, his more inhibited devotions somehow signifying a kind of ultimate unease with the feminine business of grief; and I have a memory too of my soft, enormous grandmother, who wore a disembowelled animal in a mink stole around her neck, nudging me at an image of flagellation and asking me if I felt sorry for Jesus.

It's a very modest anecdote, this moment in amber from a perished universe, but I used to cite it sardonically in my salad days as a proof of the silly piety of the pre-conciliar church, with its appetite for manipulative emotion and a sort of solitary spiritual shrillness. Did I feel sorry? Surely the search for social justice – the actual politics of the Passion narrative – mattered more than little, internal sentimental detonations. Mawkishness just wasn't manly. The main thing was to challenge and change the existing order. Mere pity could be postponed. It was almost bourgeois, and that was certainly bad.

Accordingly, a whole culture of personal and private melancholy, the ritual tearfulness of Catholic tradition before a brutal world, fell into doctrinal disrepute as a grander anthem of confidence in mankind and commitment to the Creation emanated from the second Vatican council. And for much of my life I was complicit with the loss of that wise wistfulness which was also a night-watch, an act of wakefulness, a vigil against violence.

Yet my granny's question, which stems from the superseded spirituality of the 1960s, continues to interrogate me long after the start of the third millennium. For the texts of the Passion of Jesus in the four canonical scriptures are indeed a training manual in a novel mode of compassion, a tutorial in the faltering habits of an altered heart; and their imaginative audacity in the world of late antiquity consists precisely in the risk they run in feeling sorry for someone who is supposedly beyond sympathy and beyond society, beyond any genetic affection we might entertain for siblings and sweethearts, beyond any civic instinct of identification we might intermittently experience with the weak and the woebegone; beyond the beyond, as we say, all together.

W.H. Auden, that sagacious Anglican, put it well when he wrote:

> *History to the defeated*
> *May say Alas, but cannot help or pardon.*

Yet the Gospels go beyond Alas to Alleluia, beyond the deft editorials of the victor to the graffiti of the stifled victim. Their point of view is a Resurrection perspective long before Easter, because they relate a legal killing as a murderous annihilation, and, in so doing, they rehabilitate all the eliminated multitudes culture has accumulated in its bid to keep the peace.

Where contemporary newspaper columns and court reports – the general consensus of fair-minded folk and the great good faith of the moral majority – recognise only a villainous presence on Calvary hill, the Gospel accounts recuperate a vulnerable person. Where the civilised world declares vileness and evil to be in-dwelling, the scriptural stories demonstrate the bedevilled and demonised individual; or, in the Biblical terminology of René Girard, they show us the scapegoat within the black sheep and the Lamb of God within the scapegoat.

They invite us to feel sorry not for some luckless chivalric celebrity who merits admiration in momentary adversity, but for a thoroughly bad sort, a bogey man and a blasphemer on the intolerable border. They invite us to feel sorry, in short, for a culprit who has been condemned by the great and the good, by the god-fearing forces of law and order, by the most venerable authorities of church and state. In so doing, they reveal criminal justice at the heart of the human community and thereby deliver us forever out of the pieties of innocence into the real reverence of irony.

Now I had been raised to have regard for the police, respect for the legal profession, and deference to the clergy. Anyone who was anathematised by all three cohorts, as Jesus had been, must be a monster on the margins. Besides, hadn't my teachers taught me that Pontius Pilate's *Pax Romana*, with its central heating system and its dual carriageways and its clearheaded brevity of speech, ranked among the major human masterpieces? Hadn't the Jesuits in my junior school acclaimed the Jews of Jesus' time as the most ethically advanced people on the planet, a divine vanguard intent on the steady sanctification of dailiness through prayerful deeds, forever alert to the hurting categories of the poor and the persecuted, convinced of the innocence of the calumniated, disdainful of shoddy idols and in deep communion with the one true God who prefers mercy to massacres?

If the world of Caesar and Caiaphas, the world of government and grace, prefect and priest, could be so massively mistaken in its means and methods, what of the little afflicted, unequal polity I lived in, that the Romans had resisted colonising because it teetered on the wintry rim of the round earth where they named it Hibernia? Modern

Ireland called itself a meritocracy, but I knew, as a schoolboy in short trousers, that in reality this title only ratified the survival of the fittest in a free-for-all. Force and unfairness were everywhere. It was a kind of regulated cannibalism. The liturgy of Good Friday lamented that openly. Three hundred and sixty four days of the year, talk of reason and the rule of law could triumph in official life, but the truth about our species and its savage mood-swings – the batons and barbed wire of our shadow-side – swarmed from the Stations of the Cross.

This is neither sadism nor maudlin. The public ministry of Jesus patiently predisposed his disciples to recognise victims, however veiled from view as enemies or opposites by the blindness of bigotry; and it did so by the simultaneous slow exposure of their own inner violence and victimising, for the capacity to pity is the difficult gift of one who has been a persecutor and has learned at length and at last the limits of mere justice. Judaism, the dear religion of Jesus, was itself an education in empathy, but the Galilean rabbi enlarged its remit radically to include categories and casualties hitherto prohibited. The revelation on Calvary continued and climaxed a three-year task of retrieval which extended full humanity, the face of the friend, to the stunted and misshapen stereotypes who people our periphery.

So the story of Skull Place is more than reportage. It is a sedimentary meditation on the content of the teachings of the Lord from the point of view of the pity and the pathos he had stealthily instilled in his pupils as a new dispensation of compassion that would recreate the love of law as the law of love. The Resurrection is the life and death of Jesus from the point of view of God, because that life and death models a divine hospitality toward human nature, entering what we exclude, engaging what we abhor, embodying what we abominate, so that every part and portion of us in the stricken privacy of our own Passion Narratives – the Pilate as well as the Peter, Barabbas and the bad thief too, the witnessing women and the bored militia – becomes legible and eligible again as fresh, forgiven, graced.

William Kavanagh writes: 'Torture is the imagination of the state. Eucharist is the imagination of the church.' Your morning mass or your six o'clock service may not always seem a seditious exercise, a dangerous vindication. Indeed, there was a time in my own childhood when it was the sacrament of the status quo and not the necessary subversion of the state we live in. Routine and repetition have diminished its counter-cultural energies, just as the stations of the Cross have deteriorated from a transcript of the truth of our society into consolatory kitsch; but the liturgy is still nostalgic for the fragility of its foundation, its fearful origin on the eve of capital punishment in a figure who offered himself as food and drink to follower and foe alike, deflecting the imitative violence of retaliatory conflict, which is the human norm, into the humble mutuality of a meal eaten in community, which is the divine nature.

However we beautify and embellish the rite of Eucharist, which marks so memorably a rite of final passage from one understanding of human nature to another, from a theatre of mortal exit to a stage of immortal exodus, an entrance into the transcendent, its documentary protocol must resolutely retain that first historical starkness. Beyond all sophistication, it is the Sabbath service of the victim and so it is the commemoration of all victims and of all victimised victimisers as well. It is the supreme sacrifice because it demonstrates that nobody should ever be sacrificed or scapegoated.

In a word, it is the Mass and not the mob. It is the perspective of gratuitous pity, of a new tenderness and altruism that will mystify the determinists and the Darwinists till Kingdom come.

So we assemble, out of the grievous, gradual lives that occupy and preoccupy us, to hear again the story of the representative victim and the story of the ministry that made his victimhood inevitable, as it would and must do today. We assemble to eat the meal that transforms our satanic appetites into human hunger and thirst, to share the bread and wine that alters those we fear or frighten into the living image of our own flesh and blood.

We are exchanging the cadaverous Roman peace for the peace of Christ, coercion for companionship, virtue for vulnerability. And already, before even Easter morning has broken and opened up the ground beneath our feet, before the rainstorm of the Passion has mutated into the rainbow of the Resurrection, already the numbness is leaving our fists and our fingertips; already sensation is returning to our terrified nerve-ends, already our hearts are beating more rapidly, like an unborn infant drumming with his heels against the bodhrán of the belly; already the salt sting of our tears tastes like medicinal antiseptic.

Already we are rising from the dead.

8.

Fables and Stables

Toward the end of his pontificate, Benedict XVI reflected briefly on the burning question of the two beasts of burden, the ox and the ass, who chew the cud contentedly in our Christmas cribs.

Now he didn't go quite as far as the Roman Catholic Council of Trent in the late sixteenth century which absolutely prohibited the poor animals from being present at the manger along with an unoffending female obstetrician called Salomé who crops up in one of the early heretical Gospels – St James's so-called prequel to the Nativity tale – of which quirky chronicle, incidentally, the Eastern Orthodox churches in Dublin, for whom the Epiphany is neither little nor late, remain fondly affectionate to this very day, even though the story of Mary's juvenile travails is not, and was never, canonical scripture.

Still, in his new book about Our Lord, entitled, rather unfortunately for an Anglophone audience, *Jesus Von Nazareth*, the Holy Father did red-line the historical possibility of the cow and the donkey ruminating together in that ad hoc delivery room at the birth of the baby boy in Bethlehem. It isn't in the account, so it can't be true;

or, at any rate, it can't be fact, since fact, particularly in its statistical forms, can now be vindicated as a supplementary source in the science of theology.

This kind of scholarly rigour about the role of figurative speech in Biblical texts is quite poignant, howsoever correct, at a time when many Christians in the EU and the NATO countries – which is to say, many adult believers in the postwar empire of the latest Treaty of Rome – are struggling with Holy Writ itself and not just with cows, sacred or secular, for that matter. In this, at least, they are imitating their Semitic seniors, since the word *Israel* is the Hebrew for 'wrestling with God', and wrestling-with-God is the age-appropriate activity of grown-ups everywhere.

Mysticism, after all, is only a high-faluting term for maturity.

Sometimes a bear-hug, sometimes a bare-knuckle bout, and sometimes a species of embrace suspiciously like edgy love-making, the blood-sport of a close encounter with the God of Jacob in the Christian texts of the New Testament does not entail either a unified Torah, dictated by the Almighty to Moses and parsed painstakingly by the rabbis, or a unitary Koran, dictated by the archangel to Muhammad and mulled by imams, but four short higgledy-piggledy biographies of Jesus in mediocre Greek whose contents can't be harmonised, a missionary sequel of sorts that's worthy of Rider Haggard or Robert Louis Stevenson, lots of letters, most of them from a former Pharisee and published in the wrong chronological order, and an apocalyptic vision called the Book of Revelation, the allegorical intricacies of which have exercised psychotics for the past two thousand years.

Here at last, in other words, is a gospel truth we can recognise – the gift and graciousness of a wealth of human writing that is every bit as complex and contradictory, obscure and tantalising, as the ordeal of the world that it interprets so hopefully.

The pope, of course, had a pedagogical point. Neither Matthew nor Luke makes any direct mention of our four-footed friends. They arrive into the stable diagonally, as it were, from a few pretty references to symbolic livestock by the prophets Habbakuk and Isaiah in the Hebrew Bible of the first Jewish Christians, but they were hugely taken to heart by the early followers of the Way. Indeed, the two animals were being carved on stone sarcophagi in the fourth century, before the figure of Our Lady ever appears in the frame, or in the frieze – seated, be it said, and not supine, in order to emphasize the breezy ease of her labour as the soft accomplice of Providence and the mother of God. Back then, the ox would also have signified the Jews, oppressed supposedly by their own morose legalism, while the ass in turn typified the gentile converts with their docile choice of a lighter yoke in the plain man's Galilean agenda, although nowadays you'd need some high-church prelates on your pub-quiz panel to retrieve such ancient and obsolete intentions.

Francis of Assisi, who fashioned the first domestic crib for the late medieval proletariat of Umbria as a straw-and-wattle substitute for the stained-glass windows of urban chapels, underscored store-cattle and sheep at the solstice scene in order to earth the Incarnation and to foreground the humble grandeur of God's creation in the comfort of local detail for the sidelined illiterates whom he served.

That thirteenth-century impulse – to turn chalices into cups (which is what chalice means in ancient Greek) for his thirsty and impoverished parishioners – was a pastoral critique of the current liturgical tendency, judging from the revised Roman missal, which is to turn cups back into chalices in a bid to overly solemnise the everyday nature of the sacred and to restore its previous, precious élitism.

Francis understood, by contrast, that the closer we are to the world, the closer we are to God. In this, he and his contemporaries critiqued the thinking of a thousand year-old theological aversion and helped to inseminate the Renaissance. Husbandry of the universe discloses the holiness of the here and now; or, in the terms of the mythology we call the standard model, which is modern scientific rationality, it did not take the Word of God nine months to assume flesh in the womb of Mary. It did not take even thirty three years in the more spacious timeline of the world. Instead, it may have taken thirteen billion. And that is not just history or pre-history – it is, as the French say so wisely, an *histoire*, a love affair of longstanding.

Which is to say as well that the wooden ox and the ass I bought in a shop called Nimble Fingers three intricate decades ago, and which this morning decorate an inherited hunting table at the front door of our home in Dublin, are invited in this or any Year of Our Lord to embody a novel hospitality – novel, at least, to someone like myself, a city spiv, an office worker who has never slaughtered any of the food he devours, and is therefore guilty of a truly terrible innocence, even if he sometimes wonders what his Sunday roast would make of the Christian Grace before Meals.

They are invited, the moocow and the mule in the pure filth of the primal shed, to express the dignity of our collaborative origins in the fellowship of all physical life, in the sodality of the temporal realm, and to trace the sacrament of the human to the slow and subtle impetus of a spirit that blesses and saves all the ages and stages of matter.

Mind you, I make it all sound far too po-faced, and that's because the mind itself is material, in its many shades of grievously grey matter, and therefore always and everywhere inadequate to the task of Technicolor joy. The million and more viewers who've watched the YouTube video-clips of a pole-dancing brown bear in the Canadian forests or the mother-daughter bond that formed between an elderly giant tortoise and an orphaned baby hippo in the slipstream of the tsunami, laughed – or, at any rate, howled with laughter – because mischief sees what melancholy misses and what the prophet Isaiah himself envisioned in his talk of lions and lambs, let alone donkeys and dairy cows: that in the whole, humanitarian world, there's a sediment deeper than divine tragedy, and that warm bedrock, that base beyond everything, the angelic aspect of the apex predator, is divine comedy. Even our fasts are festive. My own dad, Lord have mercy, thought he'd lived to see everything, like Simeon in the sanctuary, when he watched Bing Crosby duet with David Bowie at a baby grand piano on MTV.

Perhaps when he put the two beasts of Bethlehem back in their Old Testament paddock, the pope as a senior exegete momentarily omitted to remember what the second Vatican council (of which he was an important part) stressed in its humanitarian sanity. It is not always enough for the Word to become flesh; it must become fresh as well.

Over almost two millennia, we have been adding and subtracting from the Nativity story, just as the evangelists did in the first place when they edited and/or invented the traditions. For the opposite of fact is not necessarily fiction. It is often the elucidation of truth, which is the nature of all narrative. Saint Augustine was troubled in his time by the lack of any reference to the Flood in the historical record of contemporary cultures, and Voltaire in a later era bitched delightedly about the same embarrassing absence of any waterproof credentials for most Biblical legends. Ditto today the star of Bethlehem, the census taken by Quirinius, and the disorientated wise ones from the East whose Epiphany visit has morphed into James Joyce's use of the word as a literary term, just as the midsummer Feast of Corpus Christi has mutated into Bloomsday, the holy day of Nora and Jim, a gentle, congenital occasion in mid-June.

So the carnage caused by Herod may not be historical; may instead be Matthew's fictional *modus operandi* for a prestige parallel between Jesus and Moses, with whom God talked face to face. But it did not require the recent massacre of the innocents in a classroom in Connecticut to declare as another truth which is self-evident that lethal violence, whether genocide or gendercide, is our human monopoly, anymore than it required the death of our lady called Lovett at a grotto in Granard thirty three years ago to show us the shadow-side of the Nativity tale in the solitary terror of an unmarried mother in a Puritan abbatoir.

The fable of the stable is, accordingly, both a Magnificat and a Kyrie. It is, in fact, the *fetalia*, a word used once and once only in the entirety of Latin literature by the same Saint Augustine who had such scruples about the deluge. It means the Feastday of the Foetus, and it proposes the naked human family as the molecule of minor community in an otherwise atomised social order. Yet it also holds a mirror up to culture as the handiwork of Cain. It does this, it does that; it does the other. It does more and more, moreover. It is alive. It is changing us and we are changing it. Someone should tell the more meticulous scholars. In fact (or, at any rate in fiction), we can go on milking it forever, and we will still not come within an ass's roar of its ability to silence us.

9.

Touch Wood,
Touch Stone

Foretelling the future is a straightforward affair. You don't have to be a wizard at probability calculus or the intricate statistical projections of a mathematical trajectory on a wall-chart. I'm a Capricorn, as it happens, and the horoscopes I've read over half-a-century have always been unnervingly spot-on. In fact, forecasting is in its own way as strict a science as genetics: just as the limbs of an apple-tree will, in all likelihood, produce edible apples in the autumn, so too a blue-tit's egg will almost certainly fracture to reveal a blue-tit's chick in springtime. 'What are you going to be when you grow up?' the teacher asked my daughter Lucy when she was starting out in Low Babies, now solemnised as Junior Infants, and the child told her in a whisper, as if it were a lethal secret: 'I'm going to be a woman.'

More recently than that, a retired bishop, who taught me Plato's dialogues out of Penguin paperbacks thirty-five years ago, was touring a maternity hospital during his last diocese and he commented prophetically that the midwives knew which new-born babies would be recidivists in Irish prisons in the twenty-first century, watching the tops of buses from a barred window, and which would be the barristers who sent them there after a masterful cross-examination in the Circuit Court.

In a word, we are not altogether surprised by the inevitable, by the fullness of time, even if we are invariably amazed by the sheer stamina of the slow sequence of events that enact it.

Predicting the past, on the other hand, is a very complex undertaking; for the past, because it is omnipresent in the temporal order of things, has a limitless future ahead of it. It will not stay still for long enough to be minded or reminded. It is always molten and never moulded. Each generation will revise, if not entirely rewrite, the version authorised by its predecessor; and our own posterity will continue the practice as we turn in our biodegradable graves, dismayed by what our children's children will condemn or condone in our unexamined lives.

When I was a child, by way of example, I had two grand-uncles. One was a hero, a founding father, who had fought in the ditches during the War of Independence. The other was a West Brit sort, Redmondite and officer corps, who had served in the trenches during the Great War. Fifty years later, I am still the great-nephew of two close and incompatible grand uncles, but they have swapped shirts like those soccer players who throw three shadows simultaneously under the stadium arc-lights, or, more accurately, one man's halo has now tightened to become the other man's noose. The revolutionist is a bit of a bandit these days, more a thug than a trophy relative, while the decent veteran of the Somme has stopped being an imperial stool-pigeon and cuts a cool, chivalric figure in the third millennium.

In similar style, the white-headed boys of the Roman Catholic priesthood of my infancy, whose power and prestige modelled the insanity of all celebrity in a grotesquely genuflecting culture, have recrudesced brutishly in the present decade as a psycho-geriatric cluster of celibate misfits, while the well-adjusted, inter-relating rest of us, beating our breviaries into broadsheet newspapers, enter the promised land of secular modernity.

Pity the poor presbyters in the mud-guards and bicycle clips of their better years! Their Palm Sunday is all passion now as the old hosannas key-change into a hate-fest and the barber's chorus quick-steps into a scalping party. History may be His story, may be God's story, as one such religious always suggested in my 1960s Jesuit classroom that smelled of boiled egg and black banana, but the Western deity, the God of Abraham, whether in his original Semitic unity or in his later Christian trinity, has been targeted as a rotten and disreputable editor of dirty books, more Pharaoh than pillar of fire, more Egypt than Exodus, more human disclosure than divine revelation.

Passover, the week-long feast of freedom in the Jewish calendar, began at candle-lighting time on a Monday evening its annual illumination of the Lord who favours slaves over slave-drivers, the little trafficked victims over sexual chic; but, in the inter-Testamental era, when a libertine Galilean rabbi adapted its protocol for his own subversive purposes in an upper room in the holy city of Jerusalem, the Israelite vision had, in his extremist view of it, deteriorated into finicky fine print, sectarian small writing, the obsessive-compulsive idolatry of Torah.

That's a pretty shocking critique of the theological passage from Sinai to Sion, from adventure in the desert to detention in the dialectical back-streets, because the Hebrew cult that would graduate eventually as rabbinic Judaism epitomised the best ethical initiative of the ancient world. Paganism in comparison was mere pageantry, abracadabra for the dull multitudes. No educated Greek or Roman in the Mediterranean world took the goddesses Isis or Aphrodite any more seriously than we do the Miss Universe competition in Bermuda.

By contrast, the venerable members of the Sanhedrin who sought to assassinate Jesus were devout liturgists, devoted family men, inveterate readers of the Palestinian edition of the *Guardian* and exemplary project managers who would happily have banished any bully in their midst to an anger-management course run by Human Resources.

Indeed, Caiaphas, whom Christians demonise as a Mafiosi wise guy, is a prototype Catholic theologian. If, as he argued to his entourage, one man should die to save a whole nation, how much more so should he perish to safeguard the species itself, living and dead, and win the world into the bargain?

Jesus ultimately repudiates Judaism of the literalist kind that he frequented in his own lifetime, although he was conflicted by his own inherited tendencies in his earliest dealings with gentiles such as the Syro-Phoenician woman; but he also repudiates Christianity whenever it degenerates into mere legality, committing its own tactical crucifixions to forestall the terror of the terms of a real Resurrection.

The truth is that the human organism can scarcely metabolise power, civil or spiritual, without becoming toxic and dying in due course of radiation sickness. The subtle and gratuitous brutality of those who may boss us in our workplace suggests this to be the case, although the subtle and gratuitous brutality that we direct in turn to those below us in our demented, incremental hierarchies is only ever, of course, the inadvertent result of utter fatigue in the endless service of others.

Unspeakable violence has always had the last word in the human community, and that is why the Word of God calls out with a loud cry from the killing fields. Overkill is, in fact, our actual predicament as primates. Those who embody the stigmata, the wounds of the word of God on the cross at Calvary, are not the meretricious tricksters of the tabloid imagination with their self-inflicted scratches, but the annihilated individuals we have stigmatised, just as church frescoes and altar-stones commonly cancel out Judas, mustering eleven instead of twelve disciples at the trestle-table of the last supper – and thereby massively missing the whole point of the precariousness of Eucharist.

Accordingly, Jesus demands that we try to hybridise, however impossibly, the innocence of the dove and the wisdom of the serpent, for reverence without irony is a kind of docile maudlin towards God and irony without reverence is only criminal disdain of the Creation. But the partnership of alertness and affection can keep us from the crisis of hypocrisy – which defect is not, incidentally, the worst thing in the world. Hypocrite, after all, is only the Greek word for a play-actor, someone whose role consumes his responsibility and whose mask obliterates his face. As a matter of fact, there was one such classical theatre, two mulatto miles from Nazareth in a town called Sepphoris in the higgledy-piggledy world of multicultural Galilee where Jesus grew up finally.

I was at the theatre myself some weeks ago. The Abbey in Dublin dims its lights each evening at exactly the moment the Salvation Army hostel opposite opens its doors to the down-and-out, and I get great pleasure out of the simultaneity of the two attendances, the bourgeois playgoers settling in for a proletarian drama on a raked stage while the battered street-people tune in to some middle-class Skybox idyll like *American Idol* or *The Real Housewives of New Jersey* on the television set in the refectory of the shelter.

I had gone into town to see a play about the institutional Irish church of my childhood, its sterility and sadism, and I have to say it was very well done indeed. Had it been performed fifty odd years ago, it would have been as deep and dangerous as Second Isaiah, but the women in front of me this February night were enchanted more by its hairstyles and hemlines than by its fearless flogging of a dead nightmare.

I thought of the woman who mothered me and who grand-mothered my children, a person who gave me faith in faith itself, and whose unremarkable life was more than the ordinary handiwork of the Lord. I think she was probably one of God's masterpieces. She was also an illegitimate child brought up in a happy orphanage by tireless Sisters of Charity, those single and singular women, who cherished her just as she cherished them. Two of the nuns, a primary teacher and a poultry-keeper, survived the seventy long years of her life to pray beside her body in the mortuary of one of their marvellous hospices after she had thanked God, given me a final blessing, and turned over in the bed to die.

Then I thought of my wife sitting beside me there in Row P of the dark and perfumed auditorium, a woman who returned me to my faith when I had lost it and could not remember where, for the life of me, I had left it. She is the love-child of a teenage girl who spent her terrified pregnancy jumping off haystacks in the West of Ireland before labouring on the earthen floor of a cottage without electricity or running water which is now a wall-fallen holdall for drills and harrows, implements that signify agribusiness and the ancient, glinting silhouette of a space that is part torture-chamber and part heritage-centre.

I thought too of the County Home where she was confined, this child of a mother, this mother of a child; of the North of England factories where her contrition continued indefinitely, and of the desperate toddler in a wooden bottom-drawer in the back of a cleric's tut-tutting Ford Anglia being driven to an elderly adoptive couple on the other side of the country.

And then I thought of America where I had emigrated in my twenties to avoid the awful Calvinism of a paralysed Republic, only to discover that my friends in San Francisco, the straight, the gay and the glum, who had grown up without the doubtful benefits of clergy, were every bit as fragile and as complex in their sexual shyness as any belted

Christian Brothers' boy back home, and that the Third World students in my high-rise, high-density campus housing rushed to welcome me there with English endearments as spoken in Ireland – *Have you the time on you? Are you after forgetting? Is it me or am I gone mad?* – because they had all been exercised and energised by beloved Irish missionaries in Bogota and Lagos and Manila.

It is Good Friday on the island of Ireland. It will be Good Friday tomorrow and it will be Good Friday the day after as well. It will be Good Friday on Easter Sunday. It will be Good Friday next week and next month and next year. Not even the Gulf Stream can warm us at this time. It is truly the third hour. There is darkness over all the land, and rightly so. It is lights out, a night-crossing. We are summoned to endure the darkness as a paschal eclipse, as a profundity; and endurance, alas, indicates duration, doing hard time, the slow tocsin of the taskmaster.

This is not semantic trickery. The third hour is not momentary. It is momentous. And the third day is not a matter of three days only or of a swift seventy-two hours, a rush to Resurrection with a clockwork Christ popping up promptly among chocolate eggs and the skeletons of spring lambs. It never was and it never will be. Holy Saturday can take a whole generation to pass – and to pass over.

Yet Good Friday remains a good thing and a good time too, neither Black Friday nor Bloody Friday as in the sinister Irish litanies of our listed atrocities; and the third day too remains among us as the fullness of that time, a free and foretold future, like the vegetarian paradise of an earlier third day in the story of Creation in the Book of

Genesis in the Hebrew scriptures. In the beautiful Biblical legend, the third day is made to manifest the instant of life itself, elemental vitality, the end of pure chemistry and the beginning of imperfect biology; the green gene, generation, when our dust turns into pollen and our graveyards into gardens. Then the earth will indeed bring forth grass, herbs yielding seeds and trees yielding fruit, each according to their kind and to the provident kindness of the God who can coax our saltwater tears into freshwater streams, and the ugly deluge of our deeds into works of irrigation.

10.

Now and at the Hour of Our Birth

L et me start off, a bit like the Mass itself, on a note of cheerful confession of fault (and therefore of faith). I'd forgotten the title of this talk in the long interval of a month or more between pencilling it into the transmission schedule in November and actually setting out, never mind sitting down, to write the script for breakfast on the feast day. So I checked the listed programmes in the Guide only to discover that my comment on Christmas is described therein as a factual broadcast.

Now I'm second to none in my love of the Nativity narrative in the two gospels of Matthew and Luke, even if Mark and John aren't remotely interested in the story, but I know in my heart of hearts that the ballad of Bethlehem is an emblematic nutshell of the Easter event, a kindergarten version of the Passion, and that Our Lord was probably born in comfortable circumstances in Nazareth in or around 6 BC, six or seven years before the start of the Christian calendar.

That in itself makes some sense because an adult encounter with Jesus always comes before a relationship with Christ. We can only feel the gradual, gravitational tug of the Son of God, let along God the Son, the second person of an inscrutable Trinity, if and when we experience the wall-fallen Son of Man in ourselves and in our neighbours – which is to say, plagiarising a gorgeous coinage from Joyce's *Finnegans Wake*, in our 'nigh boors', those deplorable people who live locally and should of course be shot.

We are talking, in other words, about myths and metaphors, the holy spirit of the breath of language, the intelligible mystery of things that are signs and signs that are things, the poetry of common prose; and we are talking about a double infancy, for the Latin term *infant* means speechless and/or unspeakable as well as baby, which is why the Irish emigrant Luke Wadding over in Louvain, four hundred years ago during the penal period, spoke so prettily of the 'wordless Word' in his Christmas carol.

Whoever wrote the prologue to the Gospel of Saint John inaugurated the usage of the Greek abstract noun Logos to signify the Christ of God, the intermediate man, but there is nothing whatsoever that is logical or abstracted about the long labour of Christmas. It is utterly – and unutterably – illogical; it is utterly – and unutterably – concrete. It is Christ's Mass, a service of the world that begins in sheds and not in chancels, in lean-tos and not the perfumed Lateran.

Even those who preside at Eucharists can get this wrong. At the Advent masses of my childhood, a fresh-faced ordinand on the altar would admonish us prospectively not to neglect the spiritual side of the holy days, as if holy days and holidays weren't one and the same reality, and as if learning from a cookbook how to bake a squidgy chocolate log for your new boyfriend weren't as prayerful and as pious a work as a decade of the Rosary, because Martha too has her Magnificat, her kitchen-sink tragicomedy, and it is something else to witness.

Now the curate in the dazzling sanctuary half a century ago was a nice man who did a nice liturgy, and my grandmother, who always called the youngster Father, used to remark that his mass was 'only beautiful', and she was right about that. Certainly he held the host up for a very long time at the consecration, to the tintinnabulation of bells, so much so that you began to look at him and at the purple chasuble celebrants wore in the run-up to the *carte blanche* of the counter-culture, and not at the enormous wafer – or what a kid on Achill Island once referred to in the same 1960s as the moon bread – that he was solemnly elevating.

Of course he meant well, and the real presence in the pews – the fragile, footsore multitude of head-scarfed women and small children in short trousers, not counting the men – was too busy trying to remember the strange responses in Pope Paul's replacement missal to notice the elegance of his steepled hands and his gleaming Brylcreem at the upside-down altar of the second Vatican council.

Down in the benches we were wrestling with the matter-of-fact mundaneness of novel phrases such as 'and also with you' in place of the collar-and-tie classical formality of '*et cum spiritu tuo*'; and we were truly scandalised when the parish priest, a veteran of the Normandy landings twenty years before, told us from the lectern instead of the pulpit that we were not our spirits, and that he was only quoting Thomas Aquinas, the angelic theologian.

The laity too can miss the whole point of the arduous birth of the ginger baby out the back in bad weather. A mate of mine in a snug in a pub said to me once, in a moment that was part Eureka and part Heineken, that I went on and on too often about the body, and that all this talk was hard on the soul. Later, one of my children sent me as a candidate Xmas Internet e-card a photograph of a twenty-one week foetus grasping a surgeon's finger with its bunched, bonsai fist through a puncture in the uterus, like the contact point of the human and divine on the Sistine ceiling where God and Adam chance their outstretched arms. Yet an expectant mum I showed it to thought it obscurely morbid.

But flesh and blood is not just our bread and butter; it is our bread and wine as well. A polyunsaturated diet, multivitamins instead of grub, may be on the fast-food menu for my shocked friend's future offspring. They may live a very long time without ever experiencing its fullness. They may at least exist after a fashion without once watching their children be born or their parents die. They may bypass embryos and corpses altogether, like a middle-aged English acquaintance of mine on the cusp of early retirement, who has never seen either.

Yet I think my daughter Lucy shed some light on the weight and welfare of the stable place in Bethlehem when she called out as a toddler during a sung Gloria in our parish church: 'Has Holy God got a toilet?' Indeed, He has; and He has contrived the Creation, gently and ingeniously, in such a manner that it passes through us as we pass through it.

Here is Holy Communion under every imaginable species. Here is the physical understood as the metaphysical, the material as the mystical. And here is the cardboard Catalan crib that you find in the backstreets of Barcelona, with the so-called 'cagón' in the corner, a passer-by discreetly squatting to defecate in a sudden call of nature as the entirety of the natural order calls to its creator God, not in the trumpery of basilicas or the blare of kettledrums but in the eventual form of a foundling spattered with blood and breast milk.

In a word, we are back where we started. We are back where my father left me on a draughty golf course in a place called Parknasilla half a hundred years ago, where I had been caddying for him, carrying his clubs from one green to another in the strong spring drizzle. We had come across a ewe that was lambing in a covert, and my dad deserted me to find the farmer, leaving me a lightweight putter to scatter the birds that might swoop at any moment to stab at soft tissue. *Hic, haec, hoc* is the opening declension of the demonstrative pronoun in Latin, and *hic, haec, hoc* – this, this, this – went the tick-tock of my heart in the clock-time of crisis as my world grew vaster and vaster because it had contracted at long last into the clarity of detail and the secret intelligence of images.

The last of the baby boomers, I am nowadays more mutton dressed as ram than freshly-minted meat, and only caffeine can quicken my pulse-rate in the grand casualty department, the accident and emergency room, we call the hospitable cosmos, where our fathers have run away in search of somebody else to take responsibility.

I myself have been talking Lamb of God and gorging on shepherd's pie all my life. The prosperous post-war generation I belong to thinks it has wrought where it has only wreaked, and done more damage to the planet than any barbarian invasion or Mongol horde in history. Our poor unfortunate children won't be puzzled, in the way I was perplexed at school, by the difference between climactic and climatic.

Yet even we, the hardened criminals in the carousel of privilege that has brought us from the kaleidoscopes of our playpens in the Western counterculture to the colonoscopies of our private sickbeds in hospitals with fountains and Filipina nurses, are invited not only to repent and believe, as the Baptist exhorted us, but to rejoice and believe as his star-pupil preferred.

Yes, the statisticians of Caesar Augustus will continue their eerie surveillance and their monstrous, multiplying databases. Yes, innocents will continue to be massacred, the Herodian wars will still drone on. The night will always be another day's work. Airplanes will fly from age to age like terrible predatory pterodactyls into the tall towers. But they will also land from time to thrilling time as sweetly as swans in the runways of the Hudson river. We shall persist, in other words, in building our house on sand and not on stone, in spite of the good Galilean and his sensible soundings, yet the views will be as beautiful as Venice in the waters of *terra firma*. Maybe the hosts of Heaven won't be singing acapella over the cubbyhole where the child is born; but the Mormon Tabernacle Choir, or a barber's chorus on a street-corner, are superb understudies.

For the godsend of the Christmas story is surely this: that the Lord is enamoured – of us, with us, by us; whatever preposition you're having yourself. He loves the second-rate, the third-class, the fourth-hand, the makeshift, the mediocre, the human, the here and the now; and He can coax excellence out of its own humdrum hiding places where all the Xs are crosses and all the crosses are kisses.

So perhaps the byline in the schedule is right, and this quarter hour of confusion is, after all, a factual report and not the parsing of a fable. The bulletin from Bethlehem reminds us we are called to celebrate the beautiful ordeal of the whirling earth beneath our feet. We are urged to cherish the world, the flesh, and even the devil, God bless him; for this is our reality, this is our rendezvous, this is our restless resting place.

This is the hour of our birth.

This is it.

11.

Compassion Narrative

The so-called seven last words of Christ on the cross are a scriptural checklist of the little contradictory mnemonics that the four gospel accounts of the crucifixion insert like mercury filling into the mouth of the dying Jesus, but it's at least questionable that the poor unfortunate said anything at all during his long ordeal of execution in the municipal dump we now call Calvary.

Asphyxia is the immediate medical consequence of torment on a cross (as I believe they re-discovered in Dachau where the SS guards impaled prisoners experimentally), so a suffocating man might well have ended his life in the same state in which he began it. *Infancy*, after all, is the Latin for utter speechlessness. If this be the case, the Word of God began and ended in the decency of silence, in a call to the sufficient clarity of the inarticulate in the presence of the unspeakable. That's a useful rebuke to anyone like myself who has the neck to talk of these things when he should just shut up and listen, because it reminds us that fluency is always a form of charlatanism. Instead of being brokenhearted, we are full of considered opinion and a bit of a bibliography in case our credentials are checked.

Not that I want to go on and on about the physical afflictions of Christ on the cross. A morbid obsession with the S & M aspects of the Passion misses the point altogether, much like the boastful folk at AA meetings who almost compete with each other in their lurid catalogues of what they've done and what they've failed to do in their dance with the alcohol molecule. Pride takes many forms and even penitence, as I've found myself, can be one of them.

No, the real horror, the real hell, isn't scourges and thumbscrews. It is being thrown out of the human community: corrupt politicians this afternoon, bankers this morning, priests last night, paedophiles yesterday, homosexuals the day before that, Jews when my mum and dad got married in the year Bob Dylan was born, seven sorrowful, scapegoating decades ago. No solution can ever be final because the hunt for persons to hate is deep in our DNA. Once upon a time we would have called it Adam's curse; now we speak of it as mitochondrial Eve. Whatever the name, it is one step ahead of a vaccine, a virus always mutating.

Thus the celebrity mystic from Galilee turns in a trice from hero to zero and his entourage degenerates into a plea-bargaining pack of beasts as the man who was a throne becomes a toilet. This is what professors in high places call the sociology of reputation, but that doesn't soften the smell; and that is why the crucifixion, any crucifixion, every crucifixion, stinks, no matter how much incense we may burn around the base of the cross or how much quasi-Christian bling we buy to decorate our cleavage.

In short, moral disgust is our best disguise as persecutors and the most revolting thing about us tends to be our own pleasure in principled revulsion. 'Father, forgive them for they know what not they do,' says the lovely Jesus of Saint Luke's compassion narrative as he is actively dying in the sadistic midst of the Roman militia, but this plea for mitigation on grounds of ignorance is missing from most early editions of the third Gospel. To be sure, it may be a late-starter, a furtive scribal addition scribbled in at a subsequent period by a creative copyist who felt it was something that the Lord would have said or would wish to have said or would at any rate have generally endorsed.

Yet it's just as likely that the line was sabotaged by scrupulous gentile Christians who took the view that this instance of forgiveness was a bridge too far – and was in fact itself unforgiveable. Cecil B. DeMille's *The King of Kings*, which premiered in the 1920s in the dying days of the silent movie, would, if I remember rightly, portray the Blessed Virgin Mary condoling on Calvary with the mother of the Bad Thief, at least in captions; but such an ecumenical outreach may well have been too much for the scandalised disciples of the crucified master.

Accordingly, the primitive Church subtracted the sentence from the text of Luke for the first few centuries of the Christian era. Mercy is all very well, of course, and no one would argue otherwise, but the animals that murdered Jesus must themselves be exterminated, because, well, fair is fair. At the end of the day, it gets dark, and it should do. Besides, the annihilation of the holy city of Jerusalem, which was foretold by the Gospels only a few short years after its destruction had actually happened and was therefore historical fact, supported the pro-punishment party.

Luke, then, does his own editorial sorties to orchestrate the whole story in the minor key of divine composure. If Jesus did utter anything on the cross, it was probably the single liturgical howl – 'My God, my God, why have you forsaken me?' – which the oldest life of Christ, that's to say the Gospel of Mark, reports, and which reverberates as well in Matthew's later account, regardless of any embarrassment over the Lord's sudden and shocking despair caused to their believing communities by these two plain-spoken evangelists.

But the cry of abandonment, which would convince the twentieth century Franco-Jewish mystic Simone Weil of the divinity of Jesus, did not serve Luke's purposes in the first, and so he suppresses it. Saint John, whose Jesus glitters like an astronaut in his strange and sacred simultaneity with God, wouldn't dream of permitting this human tantrum into his play-script of the Passion. His raised and risen Christ is a far cry from the loud cry of the synoptic messiah, just as his Logos is a world removed from the wailing backwoodsman whose country accent is so impenetrable that, when he shouts out 'Eloi, Eloi!' in the grief of his orphan state, the sophisticates within earshot think he's petitioning the prophet Elijah and not interrogating the absentee Father.

It's true, of course, that John, alone of all the Passion narratives, will give us the great 'I thirst' mantra of all inebriates and of those who are dehydrated by lithium, but he does not record or invent the remark out of any shrewd sentimentality. The Greek verb *dipso*, which recurs in the Vulgate Latin as *sicco* and from which we derive our modern *desiccate*, the posh term for parched, is neither an anecdote nor an intimacy, a mere frisson for the listener, but a red thread of the subtle Eucharistic fibre that binds and backstitches John's extraordinary text, a work that has been preoccupied with fruitfulness and vines since the very beginning, when Jesus outdoes Dionysus so abundantly at the wedding feast of Cana.

But the very last word in the seven last words of Christ on the cross may be the second such sentence he is supposed to have spoken, if, that is, we observe the traditional ordering of the phrases as they were excerpted over time from the witness of the canonical New Testament to fashion a litany of sorts, a prayer-wheel whose devotional spokes were shaped by the numerical analogy of the seven days of creation in the Book of Genesis and which was cherished by the composer Joseph Haydn to the extent that he wrote three scores for its brief libretto.

Just like the word of forgiveness – 'Father, forgive them, for they know not what they do,' this second word, the word of salvation – 'Truly I tell you, this day you shall be with me in Paradise' – is unique to the gentle Gentile Luke. Indeed, the word Paradise itself occurs only once in the four gospels, and it is spoken here from the hollow of a torture chamber.

Recent scholarship suggests that this guarantee from the cross has been mistranslated; or, more pedantically, that it has been mis-punctuated. The error, it appears, is neither wistful nor mischievous. It is simply the consequence of the lack of any commas in the original manuscripts. Rather than pledging immediate or even imminent relief, the word from the cross, from an individual holocaust on a hill, is better understood as saying:

> *At this very moment, here and now, from the beating heart of this atrocious suffering, I promise faithfully that you shall at a future time be with me in Heaven.*

Now that may not be as appealing or as palliative as the conventional version, but it matches the mystery of our lived human experience much more exactly. God certainly made the world, but he made it in his own good time and not in a forty-hour week with a scheduled canteen break. In the same manner, those who are crucified today will not rise up in precisely seventy-two hours' time, and no pop-up Pentecostal propaganda should persuade us of its cartoon Christianity by reducing the fullness of time to mere clockwork.

Holy Saturday is not external arithmetic; it is internal trigonometry. Its twenty-four hours can last for years. The Lord is the Lord is the Lord. He is not a magician or a mountebank or an escapologist, like Houdini. Caricatures cannot be the way and they cannot be the truth. The Creator is at least as complex as his Creation. After all, Creation is his Passion.

Yet the flesh-and-blood reality of Resurrection as the wave-form of the world is more real than any pathologist's biopsy at a postmortem. We are frequencies we cannot ultimately fathom. By the grace of God each and every one of us has already risen from the dead a thousand times in the course of our lives, falling and failing; forming, deforming, reforming, transforming.

Our Passover may even have started before the supernatural scandal of the particular sperm and egg that imagined us in the first place as another of God's overtures, for his masterpiece is neither starlight nor solar flares nor sub-atomic particles but ordinary human beings being human – being, in fact, sons and daughters of the living God whose alias is love and whose alibi is presence; and that same process of Passover continues through our time-space and our space-time into spaces and times we know nothing of and should therefore stop talking about and start trusting in. To end our sentence with a preposition is, at least in theological terms, very good grammar. It is enough to know in our bones and in our bone marrow that the Holy Spirit of the God of Jesus is no ghost.

12.

Dying to Live

My daughter Lucy had been working as an enumerator in the 2011 census of the population of Ireland. For the first while, she was handing out the forms from door to door; then she was collecting them again to send them back, I suppose, to the Central Statistics Office. When she did her rounds in a Dublin suburb, she wore a Day-Glo flak jacket that said: Census Enumerator; but people still hid from her when she rang the doorbell because they were terrified that she was a TV licence inspector.

Now I have mixed feelings about the census. In fact, I have mixed feelings about all censuses or censi, whatever the plural of the word is. I've looked at the 1901 and the 1911 figures online only to find that two of my forebears, a great grandmother on one side and a great-great grandfather on the other, told fibs about their jobs on the census forms. The destitute carter who survived the Famine turned himself into a commercial traveller at the end of his days, and the teacher's assistant who was paid by her students' results in the Model school in Gardiner Street was suddenly a certified accountant. Well, dream on.

That was then, of course, and this is now. We no longer have to fill in questions about slate or thatch roofs or whether, God help us, we put real glass in our windows or if the toilet out the back is a dry privy or an earthen pit-and-pile sluice.

Actually, what most exercised many of Lucy's clients on her walkabout was more metaphysical than bricks and mortar. Lots of householders, young and old, objected strongly to the category covering religion. They were deeply spiritual, they told her on the doorsteps, but they weren't the least bit religious, and it was high time the census recognised this fact of modern life and got over its obsolete preoccupation with sectarian divisions. This is not Lent, they insisted, this is Spring, and nobody has told the magnolias that they shouldn't sing the Gloria before Easter. Get a life.

Mind you, they're absolutely right, these godless enthusiasts who may not believe in the Father or the Son but most certainly proclaim the presence of the Holy Spirit, preferably if they can pigeonhole her in a feminine embodiment. Spirituality is the single most material thing about human beings, as basic and bottom-line in our lives as the bacteria toiling in our bowels to recycle the Creation. Religion, which organises individuals into social groups around a shared story and a few festive events in a regulated calendar, is a natural, narrative way of understanding ourselves. On occasion, indeed, there's no great harm in it, but the New Testament nonetheless everywhere urges us to be deeply suspicious of creeds and churches because (a) every collective is a form of violence – wherever there's an Us, there is, alas, a Them as well; we don't so much unite as unite against – and because (b) our anthropocentric imagery of God will eventually deteriorate into idolatry of one sort or another. Even some religious Jews can appear at times almost to idolise the five books of Moses, and some sacrificial Christians of an old school sort can make a meal of the Eucharist precisely by not making a meal of the Eucharist.

In a word, what starts as cult can often end as occult. Sooner or later most ideals will decay into ideology. Faithfulness often dwindles into the desperation of belief, and, as a result, ritual piety – or what my parents used to call 'pio-shus-ness', a word that's never been domesticated in any English dictionary – may triumph over pity. Not that piety doesn't matter, of course, but pity is surely crucial – and excruciating – even if the Greeks and the Romans despised it as effeminate sentimentality, because it is quite literally the nature of the cross. The Gospels go on and on about this. It's the bad news, at once bleak and bracing, at the heart of the Good News.

For many of my contemporaries, of course, the Good News gets worse and worse. It's not so much that the Church has been decimated. After all, decimation is only one in ten. The Church has been quartered – and sometimes hanged and drawn into the bargain. There are many excellent reasons why this should be so, of course, although the scandal of sinful or shortfall Christians (and what other kind are there?) is probably primary in a secular civilisation like ours which seems narcotically addicted to the search for the perfect.

To be sure, the search for the perfect can seem like a divine commission, but it can also be a diabolical impulse, a search that turns into a search-and-destroy. Not that it's going to change any time soon: it is the nature of our nature to be contradictory and indictable, holy and unwholesome at the same time; to be 'flawed and loveable like every person on the planet' as the late Benedictine Basil Hume said in his wise (and wily) tribute to the dead Princess Di.

So a dear friend of mine who wants his unbaptised little children to grow up loving Bach's cantatas and Shakespeare's comedies and the Renaissance masters and the Enlightenment and the entire enterprise we call Europe (a Greek word, incidentally, that means an open face) without, however, having any exposure whatsoever to those ludicrous scriptures in the paper-thin parish leaflets at a Sunday service, imagines a world that is almost as magical as pure maths: that's to say, a world of pure silk, a world of Silk Routes, without anything as grubbily obvious and creepy-crawly as its starting point in a tiny, twitching silk-worm.

An even stranger prejudice against Christianity is particularly baffling at this paschal time, when we remember the final solution of lynch-law in an age-old liturgy of the pogrom; and that's the conviction, criminal or otherwise, amongst friends and family members, that religion is ultimately all comfort and chloroform, an infantile antidote to any adult encounter with finite reality, a soother and a blanket when we're gaga in our geriatric diapers.

In fact, the fictive works we call the Passion Narratives swarm with humanitarian horrors that do not offer any religious consolation except, perhaps, the desolation of total truthfulness. Early Christians were hugely embarrassed by the snivelling, dishevelled Jesus who, as the pagan author Celsus snobbishly complains, shrieks and wails his way to Calvary instead of comporting himself with heroic stoicism as classical ethics always insisted alpha-males should. Gnostic Christians solved the problem by disbelieving altogether in the Crucifixion as an historical event, and their disgusted incredulity was later taken up by Islam which honours Jesus dearly but denies the cross and will not Google Golgotha.

Denial, be it said, takes many forms. The Gospel of John, which we read aloud on Good Friday every year, is so obsessed with the divinity of Jesus that some second-century Christians wondered if it might be heretical. His telling of the tale is a far cry from the loud cry, from the hyperventilating victim of Matthew, Mark and Luke. John has the Lord orchestrating his own execution down to the last stately and scripted detail like a master choreographer dressing the drama in the vast auditorium at Oberammergau. The three synoptic versions, each of which antedates the marvellous, mystical gospel of the Incarnate Word, were written without benefit of the umpteen Church councils and dogmatic theologians who would correct, clarify, and categorise our picture of Jesus in the first five centuries. The person who's impaled in their accounts of this ordinary, everyday atrocity clings to dear life and to complex existence.

He is dying to live.

He does not cast a cold eye and he is not a knight on horseback, a chevalier or a caballero who ponces and poses. He is a proletarian who knows that death is the direct opposite of God. He knows that death is the utter annihilation of the individual, body and soul. In short, he is not a Greek who proposes the immortality of the spirit in the long aftermath of the withering cadaver. He is a bodily Jew who praises the phenomenon of the human person as the beautiful initiative of God alone.

Which is to say: the scattered Christian writings do not gloat over suffering or glory in it. Instead, they deplore it as evil. But they do not find suffering shameful and ridiculous in the manner in which the whole ancient Mediterranean order did. They privilege it, yes; they colour-code it purple, the most costly pigment in the ancient world, but they are outraged by it. Even John, in the story of Lazarus, lets Jesus snort and salivate and roll his eyes like a stallion at the thought of decomposition, for that is what the equine verb *brimazein*, which we translate in a low-thyroid fashion as 'groan' or 'sigh', really conveys in the original: a shock, a startled, involuntary shuddering at ghastly news.

Two thousand years of Christianity has practised such reverence and deference towards human endurance that the prestige of grief can sometimes degenerate into slickness and sickliness and schlock. But the Good Friday story is not first and foremost an invitation to imitate the afflictions of Jesus, as the Latin Church likes to think in its cultivation of conscience. It is, as the Orthodox communion understands, an exhortation to refrain from imitating Peter and Pilate and all the skedaddling disciples, and the dog's dinner of mass culture, the militia, and the righteous mob; but it's also a reminder, even in the orgies of our bigotry, that we are always beginners who can begin again, since the origins of gratitude are found in the genesis of regret.

Accordingly, I drink to Jesus and not to Socrates, to the poisoned chalice and not the hemlock cup. The poet Percy Shelley, that effervescent adolescent who translated Plato's *Symposium,* would describe the great Athenian philosopher as the Jesus of Greece, just as the intellectual Voltaire would salute Christ as the Socrates of Palestine. Whether either Enlightenment gadfly knew the other's tagline is anybody's guess. The eighteenth century, after all, was generally intrigued by the dignity and the decent euthanasia of Socrates' passing in counterpoint to the pathetic, histrionic death of Jesus. But the two departures are as different as an exit and an Exodus.

I started with the census and should end with it. To do so is a stratagem of style, mind you, a ruse, a rhetorical trick called inclusion which helps a speaker feel that he or she or it is in control of things, which is never the case, of course, for we are rivers and not canals.

The biblical census of Caesar Augustus in the book of Luke, which brings Joseph and his pregnant fiancée Mary to Bethlehem, ponders the very same point. The fable of the stable makes the serious sign of the cross over our straight lines and our dotted lines. The catholic Roman authorities of the time (and perhaps even the Roman Catholic authorities of later ages and stages) think they've read and recorded and registered every human reality that can be named or numbered, and, by God, it's a voluminous survey that would crash the Internet if the Internet had existed in antiquity.

But a baby born in an outhouse, far away from flash photography and press releases and the rational chatter of the universe, will never feature in the big talk of its small print and the small talk of its big print; and the Holy Spirit will go on doing a new thing in a new way, like the warm wind turning the pages of a paperback on a wrought-iron garden-seat out of sheer and southern curiosity.

And there comes my daughter Lucy in her Day-Glo flak jacket that says Census Enumerator brightly across her breast as she strews statistical trash in triplicate on the hall-table. The hall-door is wide open, and the dirty Eucharist of this place and time fill it and fulfil it with the honourable odours of jasmine and diesel in the month of April which is also the moon of Passover.

The slipstream of her great grandparents and her great grandchildren surround her simultaneously on the threshold of her home like the breadline at Communion. She tells me she has lived in this part of the world, this patch, this tumbledown parish of gullies and culverts and cul-de-sacs, of sudden, stunning turning-points, all the days of her life, and yet it is all new to her, it is all strange to her, it is all entirely different.

13.

Passing over Easter

As a child, I felt terribly sorry for the bad thief who blackguarded Jesus on the cross, because the only line he's given in Saint Luke's little parable – 'If you are in fact Jesus Christ, save yourself and us too!' – always sounded to my adolescent ear much more like a prayer than a reproach, let alone an obscenity; the more so since it's the bad guy on Calvary Hill who includes his sanctimonious crony on the far right-hand side by saying 'Spare us', whereas the good thief, in his last act of ingenious larceny, steals his own and no one else's salvation: *Remember Moi*. Actually, I felt awful about poor Monsignor Caiaphas as well, inasmuch as his priestly policy at the Jewish synod – 'Better by far that one person die instead of the whole people' – struck me on the silly cusp of puberty as a yellow-star, yellow-pack version of the more costly atonement theology which was, after all, a form of official doctrine the last time I had peeped at my green school catechism in the preparation for Confirmation.

But it was grim, god-awful Gestas, for that is the snarling name awarded to the bad thief by the Gospel of Nicodemus centuries after his crucifixion in the Gospel of Luke, who seemed to summarise my own prudential prayer-life as a secondary school student, because, when I cut to the chase through the holy protocols of my petitionary arm-twisting, the plea rapidly became a please, please, became in a trice a single sentence amounting to the imperative: 'For Christ's sake, do something, God.'

Of course, I knew about 'According to Thy will' and all that, but who was awake to hear Our Lord utter such a principled disclaimer in the garden of Gethsemane on the night of his rendition, apart from Luke's inevitable ministering angel; because Luke adores ministering angels. To be honest, he has a thing about them. The apostles, after all, presumably were comatose and even catatonic witnesses, since, as I would learn somewhat later in life when the Passion Narrative was finally translated into the sort of Dublin English I could understand, there is nothing as exhausting as the state of terror – and, next to the expression 'Care in the Community', 'According to Thy Will' must be the most terrifying clause in any verbal contract.

Besides, it didn't need Monty Python's *Life of Brian* to remind me that an itinerant rabbi preaching from a small dinghy anchored off shore, and trusting the acoustic of lake water, rather than the face of the deep, to carry his words to the Galilean rabble on dry land opposite, would be mightily misunderstood from time to time. The world we live in is not, thank God, always and everywhere a natural auditorium for the hard Word. 'According to Thy Will' is often, paradoxically, an impossible ask.

My plea-bargaining practices exemplify a more general culture of hugger-mugger card-playing with the supreme power – what used to be called full and frank discussions (but are currently described as robust exchanges) with the God of Abraham. The habit is so endearingly human, indeed, as to be generic to our nature and genetic within each one of us. It isn't a bygone age since a mother I knew went off in search of a bloodstained mitten of Padre Pio's to counteract her pancreatic cancer, and it isn't a vanished era since a daughter I met became addicted to Saint Gerard Majella, patron of pregnancies, stowing his laminate snapshot in her nightie under a Habitat pillow, as a key element in a clandestine campaign to increase and multiply. Yet that which is childlike is not necessarily childish, still less infantilising, and my emigrant brother's eight-hundred-and-fifty kilometre pilgrimage, on two brand new silicon kneecaps, from the Pyrenees to Santiago de Compostela, is no more surprising in a secular psychiatrist who specialises in PTSD than my own distracted detour as a post-grad student of anthropology to St Patrick's Purgatory on Lough Derg in a time of meltdown and mayhem.

The copybooks in the lady chapels of Anglican cathedrals are full of handwritten requests in bruised black-and-blue ballpoint, autographs of anonymous anguish with the clarity of oriental haiku, cries from the breaking heart that break and enter, enter and break, us, the furtive, tearful voyeurs; and once, when about to rehearse a routine broadcast mass of healing in the oratory of a children's hospital, I mistook what I thought to be the tenor line of a medical choir that was forming in the front pews. They were, in reality, grown men down on their knees imploring another, suddenly alien, suddenly absent father, the God we still call Abba in the baby-talk of Hebrew, to spare the massacre of their innocents.

Now the double-trouble of human grief, however good such grief may sometimes be, consists in the fact that it is both contagious and, at the same time, incommunicable. We can share but never shed it. The Passion Narratives in the four Gospels obviously preoccupy themselves with this sad animal quandary of ours, but it's also probed in Saint John's solo telling of the story, whether it be reportage or fable or a bit of both, of the raising of Lazarus.

One of the evangelist's many concerns in this, his eleventh chapter, is to distinguish between Resurrection on the one hand and merely returning from the dead on the other, since it's important to him, and to the other early Jewish Christian communities of the primitive church, that we don't confuse two such materially different occurrences. The resuscitation of Lazarus may look in an easterly direction, but it is not in any way the event we call by that good old Anglo-Saxon word Easter.

For that very reason, perhaps, pain proliferates at the chamber tomb outside Bethany village. Everybody's crying to high heavens here, Martha, her sister Mary, the entourage of mourners, because the high heavens themselves seem unutterably remote from the reality of their recent loss, and the stench of death has put the fear of life into all of them – and, incidentally, Saint John's word for stinking is *ozein*, which gives us today's ozone, since, according to the scientists, anyway, the ozone layer reeks like incinerated steak or a charcoal cadaver.

Some of the bystanders engage in a more seemly style of keening; that's the genteel implication of the verb *klaino*. Jesus himself, however, is weeping – and no wonder, by Christ, as James Joyce once remarked – in what is usually cited as the shortest verse in the whole New Testament, apart, that is, from 'Rejoice exceedingly'; but the term *dakruo*, which Saint John chooses to describe the Lord's breakdown at the graveside, is a more ghastly business than mere commercial hullabaloo for a deceased customer by a professional honour guard. It is the nasal secretions stage in personal misery, when the face collapses like a badly made cake, and the eyes produce a slobbery, saline liquid more like mucus than the decorum of a tear-drop.

But there's still more to come from the author of the fourth, surprising Gospel, whose Eucharistic vocabulary already includes a Greek verb that we translate faintheartedly as *eat*, but which in its muscular intention is closer to the homely idiom of *munch*. As Jesus approaches the cave-mouth where the corpse of Lazarus has been shuttered, he acts or re-acts or abreacts in a strange expression. The Authorised Version gives it as 'groaning in himself', the Knox translation of the Latin Vulgate prefers 'sighed deeply', while the Jerusalem Bible elaborates the moment more dynamically to make of it 'in great distress, with a sigh that came from the heart,' which I rather like from my schooldays in the twentieth century because it brings me back without bringing me down.

None of these attempts at the third person singular aorist *enebrimésato* or its masculine participle *embrimómenos*, however, can quite take the bull by the horns, or, in this instance, the horse by the ears, since the term is originally equestrian, or, more accurately, equine, and denotes the startled snorting of the stallion, the flared nostrils of flight and fright. You don't have to be charged by a foaling mare which towers above you in a salivating fury, as I once was in a previous life, to be struck by such flailing.

Jesus, in other words, rears up in horror at each and every individual holocaust. By implication, the God he proclaims, neither passive nor impassive, is traumatised by human unhappiness. This is not fancy talk; this is not local colour in a literary fiction. This is the down-and-dirty horse sense of a scripture that is sacred because it honours the facts of life.

In the fullness of time, the first precarious Christians of late antiquity would cherish the memory and the measure of their crucified founder as different in character and different in kind to the prestige of the Biblical prophets who had preceded him; and they would represent this revelation in narrative terms, not as a theological equation such as 'consubstantial with the Father' but as a nugget, a nutshell, in the story of the Transfiguration on Tabor, where the apostolic inner circle of Peter, John, and James witness the gradual primacy of Christ in his radiant hilltop dialogue with Moses and Elijah.

Churchgoing Western Christians heard the fable in the second week of the fast of Lent and will hear it again in ordinary time in early August when the feast is celebrated on the same sixth day of the month, mark you, as the terrible transfiguration of Hiroshima in the nuclear glare of a still more spectacular sunburst. And Islam reprises the synoptic legend in the later traditional tale of the Prophet Mohammed's night-journey to the site of the Temple Mount on the acropolis of the holy city of Jerusalem, where he mingles not only with Jesus the Messiah and John the Baptist, but with more ancient avatars like the patriarch Joseph and the proto-man Adam. Indeed, my modern Microsoft spellcheck system makes the same obstinate dogmatic point as the earlier Christian account of the luminescence of the Lord when it automatically corrects my lowercase P's and Q's in the secular spelling of ... Quran and Prophet.

'If you are the Christ, save yourself and us.' The bad thief's wistful entreaty may be the working slogan of contemporary, crestfallen Christendom, but it is not a Muslim mantra. Islam believes, after all, in the ascension of the messiah from Galilee, but not in his crucifixion, while Judaism holds out for a heraldic human intercessor in the end times. We, the poor relations of the crucified robbers, are called today not to tabernacle on Tabor in an attack of transcendence, but to build booths in the little crater of Gethsemane and watch a man sweat blood.

We are not alone in this. Peter, James and John, the same shuffling triumvirate who scaled the symbolic mountain, are really present there as a heroically historical trio. For this is not about the transfiguration of the beloved one. It has to do instead, as Maximus the Confessor told us a thousand years ago, with the transfiguration of the believer.

14.

The Strange Death of Good Friday

The tabloid headline of Wednesday's *Daily Mail* tells me that Kerry County councillors are deeply divided as to whether a crucifix nailed to the wall in the council chamber does or doesn't violate recent Equality legislation and the proper separation of Church and state. Obviously, no one in the earthly Kingdom wants a resident Tibetan Buddhist, an émigré Bahai in Ballyferriter, say, or, for that matter, any prospective post-Christian candidate for local office in municipal Munster, to be put off by such a pornographic image as that of a dead man impaled on a plank, although I haven't heard that anybody in the town of Tralee, which is the theological epicentre of this intellectual *tour de force*, objects to the statue of a blindfolded woman with a machete over the law courts up in Dublin that supposedly signifies due process and the serenity of Law and Order.

Of course, since the report of this row appears in a newspaper, I can't vouch for its accuracy, but I imagine that, like the four Gospels themselves, the story is a mix of fact and fiction, and therefore contains, as fact and fiction always do, an element of gospel truth.

Now the funny thing is that, while the death of Jesus on a Roman cross remains the single most historical detail of the drama (or non-drama) of his entire life, it has struggled from the start to be taken as seriously or as literally as it deserves to be. The Passion Narrative of John, which will be read in every church in Christendom at three o'clock this afternoon, does its devoted damndest to hide the harm of Good Friday by disguising gratuitous human butchery as an inter-galactic ballet scored by God the Father and starring God the Son. Indeed, for the first five hundred years of Christian history, the Crucifixion is never represented pictorially in any medium from marble to manuscript; and, when it does eventually occur from the seventh century onwards, it features always as a triumph and never as a torment. Gritty realism came later.

Yet gritty realism was there from the beginning. The apparent source and summit of Catholic Christian life, which is the Eucharist, isn't mentioned anywhere in the ancient creeds, but poor old Pontius Pilate is there in spades, the Lord have mercy on him and on every other shrewd and stupid bureaucrat who makes the best of a bad job in what powerful men insist on calling the real world of hard choices.

The point of naming names, even if it is faintly unChristian to put the procurator in the pillory for a single managerial *faux pas* late in his career, is plain enough. The crucifixion is vital to his followers because it was lethal for the man from Nazareth. Belief in Resurrection is an act of faith, an Easter epiphany we can't coerce or control, but the squalid killing on Calvary hill is just a dirty material datum, a thing that took place on the terrible cross beams of time and space.

We western Europeans, whether we stem from a Roman or a Reform tradition of worship and witness, are so tired of the cross we no longer notice it. It's just a plus sign on an upright headstone nowadays, a sooty lightning rod on a deconsecrated steeple, or a bit of bling in a commuter's orange-coloured cleavage on the Luas. We forget that the Eastern Orthodox Church, the other lung of the language of Christianity, has always much preferred imperial iconography, the glorious God-man Jesus Christ on his throne of purple triumph as befits a Byzantine Caesar, to the videoed cadaver of a condemned criminal in the sepia tint of rapid decomposition.

We forget that a billion Muslims piously and profoundly disbelieve the reality of the death of the Jewish culprit on a cross because the Prophet Mohammed, peace be upon him, learned his reverent love of Jesus from a Gnostic Christian community to whom the cruel capital punishment of their spiritual guru could only be an abominable libel and the devil's fib. And we forget, if I may cite my own favourite instance of the failure of our evangelical nerve, those early Jesuit missionaries who tried to interest the Japanese gentry of the sixteenth-century Shogunate in the Good News from Galilee without drawing undue attention to Jesus' somewhat sticky and ridiculous end, because the oriental imagination found the whole, unwholesome scenario of the slaughtered messiah quite disgusting – and it still does.

The legend of the patriarch Abraham cherishes the story of the three men of Mamre who turn up at his tent one scorching siesta in the book of Genesis and promise him in the course of their conversation that his psycho-geriatric spouse Sarah will have a bouncing baby. Medieval theologians liked to detect a reference to the Christian Trinity in this curious obstetrical trio, just as modern anthropologists might insist that Sarah's pregnancy at almost a hundred years of age is a mythical allusion to the cultural crisis of female fertility religions as they peaked and passed on in ancient Mesopotamia to be replaced by major masculine deities, among them the Israelite.

For myself, I enjoy reading the three strangers who show up early in the Hebrew Bible as a shorthand symbol of the three different dreamtimes that Abraham's desire has fathered over the centuries with the serum of his visionary sperm: in their chronological order of birth, that's to say, first Judaism, then Christianity, and finally Islam, the separate yet sibling stages of one and the same desert-mirage, one and the same interior delirium; the three metaphysical moods, you might say, of the first Western millennium.

In the synagogue, of course, the death of Jesus is irrelevant; both in his life and in his loss of it, he is utterly unlike the regal Davidic deliverer of rich rabbinic tradition, and is rightly rejected. In the mosque, equally, his death is merely unreal; it is a phantasm, a figment, the smoke and mirrors of a mass delusion. The real Christ of the imams is all Ascension and no atrocity. The cross is therefore a double-cross in the lunar light of the Crescent moon. It is unthinkable.

Yet the solar glare of mainstream Christian piety can be just as meagre. The awful Atonement theology I was taught as a child, which is the default position in most congregations and the stamping ground of every televangelist on my suburban Sky box, grounds its giddy violence in sacrificial thinking and a bizarre heavenly holocaust that's more interesting to psychoanalysis than it is to philosophy, more legible in the prurient murk of the couch than the plenary dark of the confessional.

Jesus did not die for our sins; he died from them. His extermination did not satisfy a transcendental vendetta by substitutive bloodletting. Instead, his ordinary martyrdom gives us a glimpse of the gentility of a God whose peace – and whose pacifism – passes understanding. Accordingly, the crucial project of the Christian myth in this, the third millennium, is to restore the non-retaliatory God, that refugee Lord, with proper reverence, and to remove Abba altogether from the abattoir of our own making.

To do this, we must inevitably revisit the way of the cross, the *imitatio Christi*, by identifying rather less this time round with the victim (an instinct that may have gone to our heads) and rather more with the victimisers (a sounder instinct that may lead us back to our beaten hearts). We may even have to revisit the scriptures. They were made for us and not us for them. They are written in flesh and blood, and not in stone. Only fossil fragments have that misfortune. So the easy eco-feminist raptures of New Age Celtic Christianity with its south-facing soulfulness, its confusion of sincerity with spirituality, of the lyrical with the literary, of candlelight with firelight, may perhaps turn out in the event to have been a satisfied, gastric smile on the face of the sated Celtic Tiger, a Pelagian daydream; and the parallel national orgy of victimhood has degenerated long since, via misery memoirs and the Munchausen syndrome of a collective cultural psychosis, into finger-pointing, the poison-pen, the demonisation of idols and the idolatry of demonisation itself.

But temper tantrums are never cool theology, and aromatherapy abhors the stench of the sweaty world. Resenting what they desire and desiring what they resent, the mood swings of the public moralists are only a stage in the ageing process. To accept responsibility for what we've done is ultimately good manners; but to achieve responsibility for what's been done to us is beyond etiquette. It's even beyond ethics. It is grace.

The child promised to Abraham by the three men of Mamre is, of course, Isaac, the narrative of whose will-he-won't-he? sacrifice on Mount Moriah in the twenty-second chapter of Genesis became the textual template for the twin types of Jewish fidelity to the Lord's inscrutable command on the one hand and Christian propitiation of God's necessary justice on the other. The ram's horn sounds on Rosh Hashanah to this day in memory of the move from human to animal sacrifice in the nomadic economy of the ancient world, and the binding of the boy is cited daily in the prefatory prayers of the Jewish morning service. Early Christians seized on the story also as a preview, a prefiguring, a coded consolation in the aftermath of the catastrophe on Calvary.

Yet the text itself is laughing in its sleeve like the sniggering Sarah who mocks her own hidden fecundity when she hears for the first time of the new life forming within her, unbeknownst and unbelievable. For the God who demands the boy's murder by his father in the rudimentary English of our everyday Bibles is in fact *Elohim* in the original Hebrew, and *Elohim*, a plural noun which takes a singular verb in the heraldic style of the royal We, translates here as 'the Gods', that is, the pagan deities, the primitive ancestral pantheon; in short, the usual Stone-Age suspects with their voodoo and their totems and their tribal cannibalism.

But the God who intervenes to protect the child, to stop the sacrifice, to stem the violence, the God who calls the boy on the bonfire a 'lad' or 'little fellow' in a tender, unheard-of endearment, is a different patron, a provident presence, a new kid on the block, a junior arrival amongst the monstrous, mythological religions of the infantile human imagination.

He is the altering god, the god of alterity, and not the god of any sacrificial altar at all. And his name is not *Elohim*. It is more singular still. It is Yahweh, a name that cannot be spoken in polite society, a name that cannot be spoken especially in polite society, let alone in policed society, in the treasured temporal sphere of penalty and punishment, of righteousness and wrong, because it is the Holy Name, the tetragrammaton, the mystical four-letter word for a love beyond our tactical affections.

All of which is neither here nor there, I suppose, when it comes to council business in the town-hall of Tralee or in the conference-rooms of any urban district dignitaries in the state at large, where the writing's on the wall, pretty much, whatever about the crucifixes. Besides, in a liberal democracy where executive and judiciary only meet at the weddings of their children and each other's Christmas parties, it's probably bad form in any part of the public square to parade an image of a tortured convict that implies the criminal justice system is itself a criminal conspiracy. Better to keep such notions off the clár for the time being.

Better by far to pass over this one.

15.

The Crozier and the Question Mark

Listening to a lovely documentary just now about the death and resurrection of St Mel's Cathedral in Longford town, I was thinking back to the bishop's crozier that melted there in the holocaust of the fire five years ago. A straight stick almost a metre long (although I think in inches still) and sheathed in a thin bronze stocking sequinned with semi-precious stones and images of Celtic Christian flora and fauna, the experts say it was a thousand years in this perishable world before it alchemised again into carboniferous soot and molecules of metal, blobs of tin and copper in the destroyed diocesan museum. All that time it had served as a pastor's staff, a shepherd's crook, a symbol of episcopal power. Now it was nothing. Now it was nothing at all.

Thirty years before the blaze that consumed the building, Pope John Paul II, who has since been declared a saint of the Church in a deft double canonisation of two supposedly irreconcilable Bishops of Rome, weighed it and wielded it on his trip to Ireland. A man who had unselfconsciously metabolised the doctrinaire authoritarianism of the

Communist regime he opposed so courageously in his own country was ultimately quite comfortable with the decor of forceful leadership. He probably hoped, given the stunning Polish parallel, that he was presiding over the replenishment of traditional Irish Catholicism, but, in retrospect, he was the gorgeous undertaker of its funeral games. The Holy Spirit of the God of Jesus appears to have his/her/its own ideas about all projects of rejuvenation.

Not that I knew this at the time, when I was on all fours in the Phoenix Park in 1979 as an enthralled twenty-something; and not that I knew anything either about the croziers which belted prelates of the Latin rite come equipped with as a sign of office. The parish statues of my Dublin childhood had long since persuaded me that the overseers, the senior chaperones in my community, must all be elderly bearded busybodies who wore the helmets of the boy-pharaoh Tutankhamun and carried enormous question-marks in front of them wherever they went as a way of querying everything and everyone in their sights. By the same token, the Christian cross itself looked more like a plus-sign to a six-year-old than the minus moment it allegedly signified.

I was small then, and I'm smaller now as my skeleton shrinks and my spine curves curiously in its own interrogatory way. It's far from shepherds I was born and raised, and far from sheep as well, although I always liked to watch the smoke of their breathing rise like incense from a steady thurible at the gable-window of my mother's place in Connemara where they sheltered in the winter nights – until, that is, she developed a horror of the microbes in their droppings and installed a cattle grid their little black legs couldn't negotiate.

In all honesty, I wasn't far behind her. An astounding allergic reaction to furred animals, from dogs to donkeys, had given me the trout pout of a face like a foetus in the era before steroids, and I was obliged for much of my adolescence to avoid the living crib, the zoological gardens, and the whole mammalian order to which I wholeheartedly belong, meeting the Creation instead at the less risky reptilian level with two tortoises of indeterminate gender in our garden glasshouse whose Biblical names – Bartholomew and something else also starting with B – were printed with pink nail polish on their shells.

I may have had a goldfish too which darkened and died and stank like a toilet bowl, but nothing cuddly and therefore choking. Even in middle life, when I carried a newborn lamb in my arms from the west door to the sanctuary at an Easter vigil, it urinated all over my new reefer jacket as if out of some historic grievance against me.

Now it may seem odd to mention the Easter vigil in a Christmas reflection, but the beautiful detail of the Nativity tale, which two of the four evangelists have invented for us, is, in its own way, a children's version of the Passion. Just as Saint John would prove to be a more ingenious theologian than Jesus of Nazareth, Saint Luke, the gentle Gentile, was a greater literary artist than his Galilean subject, although the Lord himself was no mean storyteller. Saline, shrewd, provocatively pithy, his parables have all the craft and cunning of the oral tradition, but the skill set of the folklorist doesn't begin to compare with the fluency of the wordsmith

Luke whose Gospel must surely feature in any shortlist of the most stunning artistic achievements in late antiquity, comparable to anything accomplished by his cultural peers, Plutarch, Ovid and Virgil.

Matthew's imaginings of the genesis of Jesus seem, by contrast, to be louche and overloaded, even if he does square up more solidly to the counter-tenor talk of the son of Mary being an illegitimate child, and even if the feast day of his fable, which we call the Epiphany, is liturgically older than the solstice ceremonial Luke inaugurated.

None of this is by way of disparaging the hard, enduring poetry of the report of Jesus' birth. It is, after all, the bib and breast milk of a whole civilisation. But in the aftermath of that incinerated crozier in St Mel's Cathedral, in the possible proteins of its ashes, we are called upon not only, as always, to answer the everlasting questions but also to question the everlasting answers. That is, I suppose, our indigent dignity.

Cicero thought that the word *religion* comes from the verb *religere*, to read again and again, to return unrelentingly to the text in search of a studiously restored vision. Four hundred years later, St Augustine would agree with Cicero's parsing. In fact, both geniuses were wrong, yet the notion is a pretty one.

It would have appealed to the man who stood beside me several years ago in a city-centre church at another Easter vigil, another Christmas for grown-ups. He had been dancing a slow set beforehand with the glamorous alcohol molecule, more grape than grain from the sweet scent of his breath, and I liked him for it, because an alcoholic is a disappointed mystic who understands that the knowledge of water is not two elements of hydrogen and one of oxygen. No, the knowledge of water is thirst.

So, as we renewed our baptismal promises of belief during the midnight service, the man beside me didn't only repeat the formula 'I do'. Instead, in a courteous undertone that was more reverent than ironic, he said a threefold 'I do and I don't'. Actually, he said it many more times than that, but I too am trying to shape a story here, and 'three' is more poignant than 'eight or nine'. The interest of strategic truth, same as in the scriptures, always vindicates tactical fiction.

I don't know whether my partner in the pew was making a simple point in a complex manner or a complex point in a simple manner, but he was certainly making the argument that, if we don't desire both simplicity and complexity simultaneously, we won't be able to discern the riches of either approach to the mystery of a world in which both/ and is more life-giving than either/or, because a bear hug with two arms is a bigger embrace of the other than a hand shake with one fist.

In the terms of his own whimsical tipsiness, he was telling me that those who drink from the chalice should not expect to experience the pleasures of wine-tasting. He may even have been reminding me that straightforwardly sober churchgoers like myself are the very sort of person Jesus warned us about; for, to revert to the sign of the pastoral crozier that I started with, wherever there are shepherds and sheep there will inevitably be scapegoats and sacrificial lambs.

This is not to abolish present reality, like the late John Lennon in his ghastly travesty of a song called *Imagine*.

What he proposes in that three-minute meltdown of the entire historical human enterprise is precisely what annihilating fanatics from Plato to Pol Pot have dreamed of in their addiction to the eros of zero. In fact, Lennon's lullaby could be the national anthem of the Khmer Rouge, of the Baader Meinhof, of the Red Guard or the Taliban. It is the wet dream of death itself.

The opposite of death is dying, thank God, which is what we're doing, preferably at inordinate length. It seems right and responsible to take our time at such an important task. In the meanwhile, the Christmas story, much like the X-rated version we call Holy Week or, more generally, Emmanuel, God-with-us, doesn't require too much parental guidance.

The instability of the stable suggests to us that God is actually a non-conformist and a contrarian who tolerates religion, but deplores religiosity. Idolatry, of course, does His head in. What he wants is the worship of witness. If we're urged to stand by the Church of his child, it is largely because a Christian is a person who befriends lost causes. Indeed, the care of failure is the whole *raison d'etre* of our faith. Everything else is kitsch and mousak, however precious; which is why, in Luke's screenplay, only the shepherds, the sozzled centre-city car-park supervisors of their society, all ringworm and reeking of the outdoors, get asked to the christening.

In this brave new world which is neither brave nor new but the same-old, same-old puny universe, a slovenly heaven we must go on braving daily, the pageants of Christmas and Easter will continue and conclude, conclude and continue, a glistening procession of crèche and hospice, weeping with laughter and smiling through their tears like the heroines in an Anton Chekhov drama. Asked by a journalist once upon a time for her personal opinion on the subject of sex, Marilyn Monroe, a saint who will never be beatified, said that she imagined it was here to stay. Ditto our haunted human nature with its heart beat of fasting and feasting.

There's nothing miraculous, in other words, about the death and resurrection of St Mel's Cathedral in Longford town; but there is something miraculous about the people who built it and rebuilt it and will probably build it again in the octave of another catastrophe.

They know by the wit of instinct what the British Museum discovered by a stroke of science when the ancient crozier from the diocese of Ardagh and Clonmacnoise was first elaborately dismantled in sterile conditions in a London laboratory forty four years ago, to reveal to the white-coated attendants all its *pentimenti*: the clever plates of the crook and the puncture-marks in the shaft and the nail-holes in the yew-wood at the core of the thing. So far from being original and intact, it had been lost and found, fractured and fashioned anew; it had been broken and bound, minded, mended, and mutilated, again and again, in its makeshift pilgrim mode across a millennium.

The white coats glistened momentarily in the sodium light of the lab like the albs of acolytes whose moon suits were suddenly solar.

Now it was no longer a derelict relic, the frozen crozier of a coffee-table book about the treasures of Irish Christianity in a lost apocryphal past. Now it was new again. Now it was something else.

Now it was the thing itself: the quest, the questing, and the question-mark.

16.

In the Lenghtening Light

E aster, God bless it, was more fast than feast when I was small in the mid-sixties. It exhibited, if I remember rightly (yet memory can be maverick too), a sort of sacrament of the stiff upper lip and a Good Friday rite of role-model male fortitude, sweetened slightly by the wild honey of an anti-colonial braggadocio that choreographed the events of Holy Week as a parable of age-old Irish political struggle against the British Empire. Not that redemptive violence was ever a native monopoly. It's only a century, after all, since the entirety of young Europe thrilled at the thought of sacrificial chivalry, when that well-named student Princip fired his starting pistol at the very last lap of the course of equestrian Christendom.

In 1966, the jubilee year of our revolutionary Rising in Dublin, the two national narratives, Jewish and Jacobite, dovetailed with Pentecostal zest, although my poor granduncle, a chaplain who'd survived the Somme, maintained a more austere anniversary in some secrecy, since, in a comical reversal of present cultural fashion, we were bent, half a hundred years ago, on fêting men who'd fought in ditches and not in trenches.

Myself, I'd just turned ten, a pound-shop boy soprano who'd been coached by his Jesuit music master to perform a major-chord delivery of the martyred Joseph Mary Plunkett's hauntingly homoerotic poem 'I See His Blood upon the Rose' at the ghastly green footlights of the school proscenium. Somewhere out there in the torture chamber of a combination hall-and-gym, my father, an anti-cleric who adored Chesterton, sat with the same bunched fist in his lap that would buckle tapers in their card-board haloes, ten years later, at the Easter vigils, so that dribbles of candle-grease would slop fatally onto his new suede moccasins and break my mother's heart, if it hadn't been broken already, long before.

By then, of course, the second Vatican council had begun evolving its first fragile ecology in the pilgrim village of my small-scale world, spores of pure protein here and there in the mica schist; and the Stations of the Cross, which had been the template of the climax of Lent in my childhood, had somehow turned into the novelty of the *Triduum*, a three-day wonder, a liturgical smorgasbord that sought to replace the routine light collation of confession, communion, and confectionery galore at the Spring bank holiday weekend, and even tried to compete with Christmas carols and Bing Crosby as the apex ecclesial festival.

But, back then, in the pontificate of a prince the scholastics called Pope Hamlet, a council meant the urban district mainly, and my granny down the road ranting about ground-rent. Rome, in turn, was where middle-class spinsters married discreetly if they were touching an unthinkable thirty years of age, and where my older sister, a trainee translator at a finishing school on the Via Nomentana, used to hack bits of antiquity from marbles and mosaics with a claw hammer for my personal prep-school collection of classical fragments in Ireland.

The Catholic Church, naturally, signified only the suburb's cruciform Sacred Heart structure and its smelly south transept, built by the Emperor Napoleon's wife (who endured to nurse the wounded in the Great War), to atone for the sins of Donnybrook Fair, mostly a matter of Punch and Judy, of booze and broads; where Monday, an Alaskan husky, barked on cue at the bells of consecration, and the long fast from midnight for the breadline at the turnstile parish masses caused me at times to faint with phantom shoots of pins-and-needle pleasure in my feet and hands: a weird, pre-pubertal swoon that was always strangely sensual in spite of my bad breath and the bleak rebuke from others that I evidently lacked a ministerial vocation.

There've been umpteen Easters since, upside down and right side-up, in an existence that now exceeds the average lifespan of the planetary male by a whole inglorious decade. For Holy Week in the church calendar can interact, in fertile and sometimes fruitful ways, with the intimate chronicle of one's private zodiac, such that an Easter morning may fall upon us from time to time on an April Fool's Day, so to speak, or, in a ludicrous upheaval, Good Friday be forgotten altogether on the Feast of the Annunciation, when a sweetheart's pregnancy suddenly trumps what used to be Tenebrae and is now three o'clock. Indeed, the opposite of time in our terrestrial sphere is often momentous comic timing and not tragic eternity.

So my personal passionate narrative cross-pollinates pictures of, let's say, an impromptu Eucharist in a closed hospital ward with plastic cutlery laid out beside a bulletproof bay window, but the potential poignancy of the image is protected from itself, thank God, by the two Day-Glo budgerigars perched on the dirty shoulder of the surplice of the medicated celebrant whose Feast of Priests has shrivelled into a travesty of itself on this Holy Thursday evening, that busiest time for pedicures and podiatrists, amidst the slipshod flip flops of the psychotic and the schizoid and the merely manic depressive.

Fast-forward seven years and here's your haughty correspondent spearheading the procession at a vigil mass in a darkened country chapel where chicks that hatched a half-hour earlier are running amok amongst the cruets and the enormous papier-maché Easter egg (it is a children's service) on the altar. His daughters beam at him in their Laura Ashley late-Victorian smocks. Electric light sprints across their sneakers when they stamp the kneelers. He has crossed his heart and hoped to die, has criss-crossed consciousness and hoped to live. He has even practised dying with an amateur enthusiasm. Now he is ready, steady, reconciled. He is thankful for everything. He is even grateful for his regrets, which are legion.

But the Lord has his own way of earthing such ecstasies, for the shivering lamb in the man's arms decides, with reason enough, to be doubly incontinent there and then, strewing his reefer jacket on the spot with formula milk and the gastric debris of Agnus Dei, because no one has told the nervous newborn creature that the Christian Pesach is a vegetarian banquet; that the Eucharist, which is the Resurrection of Jesus and the apotheosis of the victim in a violent universe, is Edenic as well as Utopian, looking back wistfully to a humane, if imaginary, nudity, before we wore the skins of animals in our primal abattoir, and forward with a woeful joy to the naked revelation of our chronic addiction to homicide that is hard wired in the muck of our own amino acids.

Or I think of the solemn profession of a Benedictine friend in the monastery of Simon Peter on Mount Athos, fully forty years ago, all chant and chasuble and old men droning at the glamorous Passover; but I wonder now what in the name of God I was doing there, a teenage interloper with his prestige ponytail, instead of being home again, home again, in the stink of my dying brother's bedroom, among catheters and cannulas and Airfix Spitfires hanging from the ceiling rose, with my own mother manhandling his paralysed torso onto a commode, astray in herself with an anguish that will last as long as the real, and not the ritual, Holy Saturday; which is to say, for eras and for eons and forever, the *hic, haec, hoc* of human time, until eventually she dies, and a low-thyroid undertaker stitches her lips together with pink thread from a flat bobbin in his black breast-pocket to hide the horrible Parkinsonian scowl on her psycho-geriatric face. Yet how can a woman who wept for twenty years perish from dehydration?

It is 1988 again. It is a very Good Friday, and I am doing the Stations. In fact, I am doing Jesus Falls for the Second

Time. My first-born child, a three year-old called Laura, squats on my shoulders, holding my long hair like a harness in her chubby grip, her knitted tights in a vice around my throat. There is the healing reek of cub, the deep sanity of her smells: hot breath, clean laundry, pee, and the drool of ice-pop chilling my fontanel like the stencil of a skull-cap.

Mrs Heritage, an elderly widow in a crossover apron who cleans the church, and is even allowed into the sanctuary to titivate the plaque of the tabernacle, is upwind of me at the next station, at Jesus Meets the Women of Jerusalem, with her strong scent of carbon and wet thurible, sharp silverware polish, a scalded stone sink, and the rubber rollers of the mangle in the yard behind her cottage where she strains the bandages of her antebellum underwear. The man beside her on a zimmerframe, moving with the stealth and delicacy of an orangutan in the canopy of the forest, is the last surviving son of Michael Davitt, a founding father of the state of Ireland, who lost his left arm in a cotton-mill in Lancashire in the early 1850s.

We have come this far, the child inside me, the child on my shoulder, and we are back where we began, in the church where I was baptised, it would seem, only a wet week before, by a pastor emeritus who buried sixty boy-soldiers on the Normandy beaches. We have somehow survived the reign of the prince bishops, and lost half our lives in the process. Can we survive the terror of the puritan divines in the time remaining? Now we must take responsibility for all the things we have done. That is only good manners, after all. And now we must also take responsibility for all the things that have been done to us. But that is a difficult gift,

143

as much affliction as grace, for we do cherish our grievances. Truly, they are very dear to us.

Laura looks at the Lord floundering in a melancholy fashion under the tan corduroys of a cross as vast as a hang glider. An icicle from her icepop trickles like a eureka moment onto the nape of my neck.

'Go on, my daddy,' she says to me, and kicks her foot against my breastbone. 'We seen that page already.'

17.

No Standstill at the Solstice

William Tyndale, the Reformation martyr who translated the whole of the Bible –Jewish and Christian – into salty, spoken English in the sixteenth century, was perfectly content to say that the span of a man's life is seventy years; but the literary committee which oversaw the later Authorised Version of sacred scripture, preferred the more atmospheric (and archaic) 'three score years and ten', because such an ancestral idiom seemed altogether more poignant and poetic. Abraham Lincoln at Gettysburg, two centuries later, would repeat the trick with the same rhetorical repercussion.

Accordingly, my own training in these things tempts me momentarily to discard the banality of the phrase 'fifty years ago' in favour of 'half a hundred,' an expression which one of my grandmothers, who wore her first pair of shoes at sixteen, used to cite quite unselfconsciously in her stinking scullery. Of course, she'd grown up, listening to the Gospels in a chapel of ease in Clonakilty in the nineteenth century, and knew, both by habit and by heart, that every Sunday reading of such began with the dark glamour of the three words '*In illo tempore*' [at that very time], a lovely, liquid rush of sound that sheltered a strange paradox, since the demonstrative pronoun, which is '*ille*', or 'that', has within it the Roman rigour of pinpoint precision, of absolute accuracy, while '*tempus*', the noun in the ablative case, from which we derive the terms 'temporary' and 'temping', is always a fluid and a fugitive phenomenon, never at a standstill, still less at a loss. In short, the past is as labile and alive as the present. We cannot predict it.

Let's imagine, so, that it's late on Christmas Eve, five glorious and sorrowful decades ago. A boy has been sent from the livingroom of his home out the back in the darkness to bring in coal from the corrugated coal-shed for an enormous fireside scuttle that's disguised as a chest of drawers. It may be the winter solstice, but he's wearing long grey socks and short grey trousers from his primary school uniform, and he has the fish face of the asthmatic, bulging eyeballs and sunken cheeks, the same as several of his classmates, because it'll be another ten or twelve years yet before the first steroid inhalers are mass-marketed at a manageable cost by a most holy and wholesome pharmaceutical company somewhere in Switzerland, in a laboratory that is also an oratory, a place of praise and thanksgiving for the God-given goodness of the secular strangers who are angels befriending the breathless all across Europe.

He shovels as much coal as he can carry in a big brass bucket, and he walks awkwardly back along the brick path and the privet hedge in a sort of three-legged shuffle under second-rate starlight, swapping the load from his right to his stronger left-hand side at the usual halfway point, which is a cracked flagstone, marked with a number from some sister's silly hop-scotch in the summer months; and he enters sideways through the double door of what his parents prefer to call a veranda – although it's more a compromise between a canopied porch and a greenhouse – and then he climbs some stone steps up to the great glass door of the living room he had left for ever only minutes before, and he looks in.

The whole family is before him in a sudden rectangle of soft side-lighting, all six, seven, eight of them, some squeezed together into a subsided couch, some cross-legged on the red carpet, his father already fast asleep, with his mouth open like a communicant, in the special chair for his slipped disc, and the snoring dog hogging the rug at the fender of the fireplace, its paws twitching even in a stupor, in what my mother had long since convinced herself was a complex canine dream, while drowsing, of beagles wholeheartedly savaging rabbits. And everybody, bar the family pet, is faced in the same direction, focussed, transfixed, turned towards the same, smattering light source, a beam of identical brightness, the luminous glow from the tabernacle of an ancient television set with a poinsettia on top of it, a perverse thing that was all Advent and no Santa, because, year after year, it would flower early or late, or not at all, but never on schedule, whether you warmed them with a hairdryer or watered them with icecubes in the compost.

What are they watching, the spellbound brothers and sisters, as he watches them through the glass partition, like a porthole of ice prised from a water barrel, the pond of a perfect circle held up to one's face as if it were the lens of a telescope in some desert observatory? It is almost certainly a Western or a war movie. It's too late in the day for Bishop Fulton Sheen's seasonal salutation, and too early in the evening for a foreign film with subtitles and occasional cleavage. Perhaps it's *The Password is Courage* or *The Hallelujah Trail* with Burt Lancaster and Lee Remick. Maybe it's *The Longest Day* or *The Last Frontier*, starring Victor Mature, a movie with images that are oddly elongated on the small screen, because it was shot in a new-fangled form called Cinemascope which is too vast and vertical for the horizontal hold of the ordinary Irish viewer. But whatever it is, the chubby little child who will become his sweetheart and his saviour in the unimaginable future of what is already destined in detail, will be watching the same programme at the same time with her own adoptive parents in an adjacent suburban parish, because there is only the one station and the one signal, unless the breeze blows strongly from the East, bringing intermittent silhouettes from the British BBC that are as shadowy and sacred as the sepia face in the folds of the Turin shroud.

If this single glimpse of the finite world were to survive its own dazed nostalgia for a gaze into tender eternity, the boy with the coal bucket would see through the window of the garden door into the livingroom from the blacked-out glass gazebo where he has suddenly stopped, transfigured. He would discern the photographic negative beneath the smuts and stains of the soiled sheets and the dirty linen that the Catholic tradition secretes high in the sanctuary of a North Italian cathedral. He would see the unhappy

emigrant in the big-boned brother with the Cadbury's
selection box on his lap; he would see his sisters too, one
with the beehive hair-do that will swerve in twelve month's
time into a beatnik London look, the other a tiny tomboy
at her high-heeled sibling's feet, and both of them serenely
unaware, like every other phantom presence on this long
and lavish avenue that runs from a cross-shaped church to
a cruciform level-crossing, of the intricate crucifixions and
the versatile, eventual Easters of each and every human
existence. He would see his mother's face lose all expression
in the mummified death-mask of Parkinson's disease as her
favourite, first-born child dwindles into a smelly invalid;
and he would see the beloved dog that will be put down
when its bite proves worse than its bark. He would even
see himself, the boy bringing in fuel for the fire, under lock-
and-key in a quiet facility with a fountain, where the toilets
cannot be sealed from the inside, and the only other sound
is the castor of the medicine trolley, like the rhythmic tinkle
of an ice-cream van in the corridor.

But he would also see the children's children; and
theirs again. He would see the great-grandchildren, even,
the sallow son of a Baghdad beauty here, the oriental
offspring there, the multiplying image and likeness of the
livingroom in Melbourne and in London and Vancouver
and Calcutta, humming as they wash and breaking into
song, the full-throated signature of our species and not the
territorial threatening of the dawn chorus, but true praise
and thanksgiving, in the minor chords of a current hit in
the charts or a classic from Abba. He would see, in short,
a genealogy as ludicrous and irresistible as the ancestral

lists in Luke's teeming Nativity. He would see his wounded, wall-fallen brethren dying and rising, and dying and rising, and dying and rising again. No wonder the boy with the coal bucket blesses himself with his frozen fingers at the glass door he is staring through. He has only ever blessed himself in the open air outside the precincts of a church after prayers at a graveside; but this solstice moment in a dark December, this stationary flash in a Dublin dwelling, is the beatific vision.

It is not enough, of course, to wish you a happy Christmas. There is too much grief in the joy of it to excuse such pleasantries. But it would be churlish to wish you an unhappy Christmas, because there is too much joy in the grief of it, to justify such social spite. So it may instead be best, or, at any rate, better, to wish for each and every one of us in the risk of listening and the task of language, that Christmas may happen in our lives, both as feast and as fast, not only now, but elsewhere and often, or as often as we can bear it, which is probably once or twice in a lifetime. Christened or not, sheltered or exposed, we are all of us the children of the crib, fragile but not forsaken, in the makeshift magnificence of our being; because that little lean-to is our most natural habitat and our most hospitable home, where we are haunted by the holy ghost of our own God-given humanity.

For the birth at Bethlehem did not just come to pass; it came to stay.